To Kenn

from Sweet Bird Jeg
6/8/2007

TO:_____

FROM:_____

Love Letters
of a
Lifetime

Love Letters

of a

Lifetime

ROMANCE IN AMERICA

HYPERION

NEW YORK

Lifetime

Compiled by Bill Adler Books

Copyright © 2001 Lifetime Television

Library of Congress Cataloging-in-Publication Data
ISBN: 0-7868-6705-1

FIRST EDITION

10 9 8 7 6 5 4 3 2 1

Contents

CONTENTS

vi
♦

CONTENTS

Foreword

BY DANA REEVE

The first love letter I ever received was in the form of a thickly folded wad of green construction paper slipped secretly into our mailbox by the boy down the street. It was the summer before third grade, but I remember the moment of discovery as if it were last week. The contents of the letter are less vivid in my memory—something about my admirer "liking" me and thinking I was "pretty" and "nice"—but the feelings that came over me as I unfolded the wrinkled missive and read the penciled scrawl of my eight-year-old classmate burn as brightly in my memory as they did on my cheeks that summer afternoon. I was awash with waves of surprise and embarrassment (of course), but also with an overwhelming sense of awe and wonder.

It was not simply the titillation I felt at the thought of being someone's chosen object of desire that filled me with awe. It was that, even as a child, I think I recognized the immense bravery inherent in the act of writing down one's deepest feelings and giving them to another human being. How very bold to open up one's heart and soul, exposing the contents for all to see.

I was aware on some level that my young suitor had made himself vulnerable to any manner of responses. Not only was he in danger of rejection from me, but had I been a different type of person I could have quite easily set him up as an object of ridicule on the playground.

In the end, I did nothing of the sort, but, alas, the feelings my little neighbor expressed were not mutual and his love went unrequited. But his note, so carefully and thoughtfully scribed, did have an impact on me. The memory of his love letter—as simple and childish as it was—lives with me still.

Although I am happy to be able to say I have received many love letters since—and I daresay far more eloquent and passionate ones—my first innocent love letter marks, perhaps, the beginning of my understanding of the power of the written word.

A letter by its very existence is a physical, tangible mode of expression. A conversation disappears as soon as it ends, lasting only in memory. A letter not only expresses how someone feels at any given moment, but also provides a record of those feelings, a reminder, and an emotional trigger. And as my family and I discovered over five years ago, a letter can also help heal.

On May 27, 1995, our life was, in an instant, inexplicably, unalterably changed. It was Saturday, Memorial Day weekend, at a few minutes past 3:00 when my husband, an experienced rider, fell from his horse while jumping a fairly routine fence and sustained a spinal-cord injury. Chris was paralyzed from the chest down and unable to breathe. As he was thrown from his horse, we, as a family, were thrown into a world we had only glimpsed as passersby: a world of loss and suffering, hospitals and emergencies. We left an able-bodied existence full of privilege and ease and entered into a life of disability, with all its accompanying restrictions and challenges. We went from the "haves" to the "have-nots." Or so we thought.

What we had yet to discover were all the gifts that come out of sharing hardship, the hidden pleasures behind the pain, the simple joys revealed when the more obvious treats and diversions that life has to offer are taken away. Something miraculous and wonderful happened amidst terrible tragedy, and a whole new dimension of life began to emerge.

*All over the country and the world people
began to respond to Chris's injury. Letters
started pouring into the mailroom at the
University of Virginia Medical Center, where
Chris was being treated. Thousands of letters
a week.*

Thus begins *Care Packages: Letters to Christopher
Reeve From Strangers and Other Friends,* a book I wrote
which includes a collection of some of the letters we
received after my husband's accident. Most of these letters were not from friends, and yet they were acts of
friendship; they were not prescriptions for medicine,
and yet reading them helped us heal; they were not love
letters, and yet they made us feel loved. The letters had
tremendous power. They provided solace and became a
source of strength. As a family, we read some of the letters over and over; they became tools to elevate our
moods or fortify our spirits to face another day. These
letters were, in fact, so essential to Chris and the family
during the healing process that I knew they needed to be
shared.

So, too, do the letters in *Love Letters of a Lifetime*
call out to be shared. As you turn the pages and read
these letters, you will see that each one tells a story,

whether it is through the innocent, impassioned words of the newly love-struck or the deeply resonant expressions of a love that has endured through the years.

Many of the letters will delight you with vivid and descriptive passages. For example, when Heather Lott writes to Peter Lloyd, a boy she only recently met, the passion of her prose declares "I love you," even while she is too afraid to actually say it: "I feel the words curling on my tongue over and over but I'm afraid of them. You're near me and I feel the words circling inside my mouth but I swallow them. I'm poisoning myself with denied confessions and repressed declarations." And, although Peter's response is in a very different style, his letter expresses feelings which are equally ardent: "You know what you make me feel like? You know those freezing cold mornings and you can feel the chill on your face but your body is so soft and warm. So you put your head underneath the covers so your entire body can feel that way and then you feel like you just want to melt into the sheets and stay there forever. That's how I feel with you."

There are delightfully funny moments of sweetness and honesty, as in this note from Bart La Bar to his wife, Flora: "My dear sweet bride— A note to tell you that I love you more today than the day we married. . . . And as each day, month, year passes, your beauty and my love for you grows. I truly hope you will forgive me for my minor transgressions, such as buying 215 paperback books. There really are some good ones in this batch."

There are poignant letters of love lost. The unfinished letter of a soldier to his young wife written at the height of World War II begins to reveal his thoughts on their relationship, when duty calls: "I'd like to write more on this subject but we have to save it for my next long letter for as you will now guess, we're on tonight." The next letter his bride would receive begins, "As you will read this only if I am killed . . . I want you to know that you are the only true love of my life. . . ."

As we read the letters, there emerge lessons to be learned. Lessons about appreciating what life has to offer before it disappears, lessons about being brave enough to say "I love you" before it's too late. Some of the letters teach about the work it sometimes takes to keep a relationship together while some present examples of relationships that have endured hardship and the test of time only to grow and mellow into a life of easy companionship.

The letters may remind us of our own lives—how, for example, a first love never dies completely. Or letters of our own, with words so powerful they could only be written, not uttered. And sometimes written but never sent.

Each of these letters is a gift, as all love letters are. And, like the crudely wrought note I received those many years ago, they are gifts not so much because of what they say as because of what a written letter means. Whatever the content, they are treasures, records of personal history, or possibly even the only tangible memories of a loved one lost.

What ties them all together—indeed, what ties all love letters together—is the bravery of expressing and documenting such powerful, raw emotion. Some letters are more articulate than others, more beautifully written or more deeply inspired. Some will break your heart, while others will make you laugh. But I daresay *all* of them will engage your imagination on some level.

And, too, let's be honest, there is something deliciously pleasurable about the privilege of reading someone else's mail; being privy to someone else's love life! The following is a note *I* wrote to my husband, Christopher, on the occasion of our fourth wedding anniversary, eleven months after his riding accident. I include it neither because it is the finest piece of writing nor because it contains any particular insights. I certainly didn't write it with the thought that it would someday be published. No, I include this small letter because Chris asked me to. For him this letter was a gift, an affirmation, and a spark of hope in a time of darkness. For me, it was quite simply an expression of the truth:

> *My darling Toph,*
>
> *This path we are on is unpredictable, mysterious, profoundly challenging, and, yes, even fulfilling. It is a path we chose to embark on together and for all the brambles and obstructions that have come our way of late, I have no regrets. In fact, all of our difficulties have shown me how deeply I love you and how grateful I am that we can follow this path together. Our future will be bright, my darling one, because we have each other . . . and our young 'uns.*
>
> > *With all my heart and soul I love you, Dana*

I hope reading *Love Letters of a Lifetime* prompts you to rustle through your attic or dresser drawer or shoebox—wherever you keep those notes you've lovingly saved or perhaps just never could bring yourself to throw away. What you find there may surprise you, delight you, cause you sorrow, or provoke laughter. Perhaps there is a wadded bit of green construction paper in *your* past as well. Whatever you find, and whatever you feel, there is little doubt you will feel *something* and very likely you will be bombarded with memories. And maybe, just maybe, you will even be inspired to write a love letter of your own.

When a man goes away to war, there are many kinds of letters he can write home to his girl, sad and lonely letters, keep-up-a-brave-front letters, just-the-facts letters, funny letters, passionate letters . . . Some men can cover most of those in the course of a single long letter—and still have the imagination to spring the occasional real surprise.

Requisition for Love

John Curry and Ruth White first laid eyes on each other in an elevator in Houston, Texas in 1941. She was a secretary at an oil company, and he had his own small insurance company. Since they worked in the same building, they kept running into each other in that elevator. Mostly they talked about the extreme heat and humidity of Houston, but they laughed about it. John liked Ruth's sense of humor, as well as her looks, so he finally invited her to lunch. He took her hand in the middle of lunch, and, as Ruth would later tell their son, Jim Cannon Curry, she was convinced that they both knew, right then and there, that they were meant for each other. It was Jim who provided the letters for this book.

They were on the verge of getting married when America entered World War II in December of 1941. John realized his draft number could come up at any time and decided to enlist immediately. They made this tough decision together. Marriage would have to wait, but surely, with America in the war, it wouldn't last that long. In January of 1942, John was off to the Naval Training Air Station in Norfolk, Virginia. And the letters began. They both wrote every day, but only John's sur-

3
♦

vive—their son Jim doesn't know why, but actually that's quite common in terms of World War II letters. The men didn't have any place to store letters, and they didn't want to leave them lying around for other men to read.

John's letters began with salutations like "Dear Darling Baby Doll," and "Sweetheart, Darling," although sometimes he made it simple and just addressed Ruth as "Darling." Right from the start his letters were filled with passion, to the point of being quite racy for the time. Here's part of what he wrote on March 28, 1942.

4
•

When you write and I get you on my mind, I think I am going to go crazy for the want of you. God how I would like to hold you at this moment. It is rather difficult to describe how empty you can feel without someone. But you know that you mentally keep reaching for them and just seem to grab space. What bliss we do enjoy sometimes and fail to appreciate the fact that it is happiness!

You know, sweet, all great deeds are inspired by the emotions of sex. That is the power of attraction, and love for a woman is manifested in the acts and accomplishments of the doer. In every single instance of men

*who have done worthwhile things, you will
find the stimulating influence of a woman. I
really believe that. With your love I should
become a mental marvel!*

John also liked to tell risque jokes in his letters—
risque for the time at least. "Once there was a girl from
Lansing who was persuaded three times by her handsome. Then she said to her friend, Let's do it again,
and he said, Honey, my name is Simpson, not Samp-
son." But that was just one side of John. In the same
letter, he would tell Ruth in detail about his training,
discuss all the doings of relatives and friends back
home that she had sent him news of, recommend
magazine articles, and talk as much as possible about
how the war was going without running afoul of the
military censors.

But his love for Ruth was never far from his mind.
On April 4, 1942, he got hold of an official Navy Stub
Requisition and filled it out with a very unusual inventory request. In the left-hand column, where stock numbers were to be entered, he typed, "Only One Pattern in
Stock, Marked Ruth." In the column for quantity required, he typed "All." Under unit price he wrote "Money
Cannot Buy." At the bottom, in the issued by box, John
wrote "God." Date: "1916." Priced and posted: "Never."

5
•

In the central portion of the requisition slip, under description of article, he typed:

> *Beautiful young girl, about 25 yrs. old, brunette, exceptionally well-built, soft yielding lips, eyes like twinkling stars, hands—well awfully warm and friendly, personality—lots of, voice—soft rising contralto which tingles your spine, friendly type everyone likes. Can best be located by looking for three fingernails lost digging in garden.* (HANDLE WITH CARE AS IRREPLACEABLE & SHIP IMMEDIATELY.)

6
•

John signed and countersigned the requisition slip and sent it to Ruth. It would be a while before the requested "article" would be delivered. After completing his training, John was issued a certificate stating that he was now a "Storekeeper Second Class," and was assigned to the *USS Acella* out of San Francisco. Finally, at the end of 1943, neither he nor Ruth could stand being apart any longer, and she made the trip to San Francisco when his ship was in port for a brief layover in late November. Ruth White became Mrs. John Curry, signed, sealed, and delivered at last.

A love letter can take a great many different forms. It can be a poem, of course, and prose too can be poetic, as well as simple, direct, and quietly reassuring. But some people have a gift for turning unexpected kinds of words into a love letter. Can you make a love letter out of a list of things to do? Of course you can.

It's the Little Things

As fall slowly turned into winter, the dipping tem-
peratures forced them to take shelter. Instead of their
usual stroll around the park, Bernie and Kathy now sat
in the car listening to the radio. It didn't matter where
they were—they just wanted those few hours alone. It
had been this way for a few months now. Kathy driving
to the park between leaving work and collecting the kids
from school, Bernie altering his schedule to be with her.
It was a friendship no one could have predicted. Though
Kathy's marriage was collapsing and Bernie and his wife
were legally separated and lived apart, they were both
still married. Kathy could have never predicted that at
age thirty-five she would be having the time of her life
just sitting in a car, on a park bench or in a coffee shop
with a man more than thirty years her senior. Nor
would she ever have predicted she would be falling in
love with a former patient. But it was happening. For
right then, Bernie leaned over and kissed her.

In a hollow marriage, Kathy Thomas had thought
about divorce more than once. But every time the *D*
word popped into her head, a feeling of guilt overwhelmed her. She didn't want to put her children
through that kind of stress. At the same time, she

couldn't deny that any feelings of romance she once had for her husband had long since died. Eight years into their marriage, her husband had broken his vows. Even more upsetting than finding an eighteen-year-old blond in her bed was the excuse her husband gave her. "You never pay any attention to me," he had said, making it seem as though his actions were her fault. Kathy, a cardiac nurse and mother of two, had given as much attention to her husband as she could between work and carpools. Even in the beginning of their relationship, he had never been terribly romantic and throughout their marriage he had never done his share around the house. There were days she would get so behind in housework that her mother would come over to help fold laundry. Her job was full-time, her youngest child was still in preschool, and her oldest needed to be driven to baseball practice and chorus. Time was a scarce commodity.

There were the gray days when she believed her husband's accusations. Maybe she should have made more time for him. He was her husband, after all. Maybe she hadn't been loving enough, giving enough. Other times she thought his allegations were absurd. How could he blame her? She hadn't been the one with a lover. Why didn't he take responsibility for his actions? This wasn't the kind of relationship she wanted her daughter to see and her husband wasn't the kind of man she wanted her son to become. Once while walking with a girlfriend, Kathy turned and asked, "Is this all there is?" Although she was unhappy, she was so determined to make their union work she never told anyone about her husband's infidelities except the marriage counselor they had begun seeing. And that wasn't working either.

Kathy made the rounds at the hospital, checking on patients, administering medications. A new patient had checked in that afternoon. When she walked into the room, the patient politely stood to greet her. Looking up from her clipboard, Kathy had to laugh. He was in the hospital, it was not a time he needed to mind his manners. But that, she would come to know, was Bernie's way. He had come in complaining of chest pains and was going through a series of tests. He was compliant with the medications Kathy gave him and when she turned to leave the room, he opened the door for her as if they were exiting the finest of restaurants. Once outside, she looked over his chart and was shocked to read that Bernie was in his late sixties. His hair was dark and plentiful, with just a hint of gray around the edges. Neither his skin nor his body betrayed his age. He also had a history of lymphoma, though after chemotherapy nearly ten years before, there had been no further com-

11
♦

plications. Thinking of his chivalrous ways, she smiled to herself before replacing the chart and moving on to the next room.

Over the following days while Bernie was in her charge, the two shared warm exchanges. He spoke of his flying days in the navy during World War II, his career as a nuclear physicist and the construction business he had recently started with his son. His chart listed his wife as next of kin though he never spoke of her and, even more surprising, she had not come for a visit. When he checked out, Kathy knew she wanted to stay in touch with him though she didn't know how. Not only did she need to keep her husband and family in mind, she didn't want to jeopardize her job. Nevertheless, she wanted to see him. She got the idea to send him a little pill box along with a note reminding him to take his medication. And an invitation for breakfast.

The morning they met for breakfast, neither was sure what they were getting themselves into. Bernie casually asked what she was having and when the waitress approached their table, he ordered for both of them. Kathy smiled nervously into her coffee. When their breakfasts arrived, they moved food around their plates, too tense to eat. Finally Kathy said, "Why did you order for me?" He answered her with a hypothetical situation. What if she didn't like the meal? If she had ordered it, then she would have to tell the waitress she didn't like it. "I would never want you in that position," he said. If he ordered it, well, then the responsibility of dealing with any circumstances would always be his. All she could do was laugh at his old-fashioned reasoning. Here he was, ordering her food and ready to accept responsibility for a situation that never occurred. From there, they relaxed into conversation. When it was time to part, they promised to meet again soon. Bernie walked around to Kathy's side of the table and helped her out of her chair.

13

Through that spring and on through the summer, they met regularly for walks. In time they held hands, though it was nearly seven months from their first meeting before they had the courage to kiss that afternoon in the car. They were afraid of each other, afraid of their emotions and circumstances. Bernie and his wife had been separated for years but Kathy's marriage was, at least from the outside, intact. Inside their home it was a different story altogether. Her conversations with her husband were limited to reminders to mow the lawn or run an errand. They'd begun sleeping in separate rooms. But every day was filled with hope when she thought of her walks with Bernie. Every afternoon before they parted, they would walk ever so slowly back to their cars, back to their lives. In the letter-poem below, Bernie sums up the happiness of their walks and the pain of their daily good-byes.

To Kathy,

Let's walk, the long way home.
Let's look for the long way home.

And on the way, let's pretend
that the wonderful walk will never end.
Through Asia would be much too soon
we'll circle once around the moon.

We could fly through the night, holding hands as
    we go.
See that star on your right, shining on us here
    below?

The whole trip it appears
will only take a million years.
So if you're in the mood to roam
then let's take the long way home.

Forever yours,
Bernie

14
•

Reading these words, Kathy knew she didn't want to take the long way home. She had found a true and meaningful love. She didn't want it to be a shameful secret filled with the anxiety of being seen, always ending in the promise of a better tomorrow. She wanted and deserved a better today—for herself and her children. For so long she had protected her children from a broken home, only to give them a house devoid of marital love. Unwilling to keep up the facade any longer, Kathy asked her husband to move out. What she found hard to reconcile in her mind was the fact that she was doing to her husband what he had done to her five years before. She talked to Bernie about this. He reassured her, saying that since she had asked her husband for a divorce, there was nothing to worry about. Still, Kathy couldn't help but wonder what Bernie truly thought of her. In his letter below, not only does he tell her what she means to him but also reminds her how important she is to others.

15
◆

My Dearest Kathy,

Today you posed a question as to what I thought about you.

Picture if you will a garden of flowers and as you walk amongst their beauty, it seems as though each group is more splendid than the last.

Picture one that really jumps out at you. That one flower pales all you ever

*conceived of as breathtaking. As you
continue to walk, your mind returns to that
special one and it absolutely brings a
fulfillment to you that you find impossible to
describe.*

*I know if we would have walked together
through that garden and I was asked to name
this beauty, it would have no other name but
"Kathy."*

*Some people come into this world
nothing and during their lifetime do the
same. Others like you come into this world
and bring with them a love and so much
happiness that it makes those around them
feel more important. I know you can't
accept this, but those around you will
accept it for you.*

*As for me, words spoken or written will
never totally tell you the wonderment and
love you have brought into my life. I've
carried a void within me for such a long time.
You and only you could have possibly filled it
to the point of overflowing.*

I have nothing but absolute love and

16
•

great respect for you. Besides the above, I pray
you will remain my best friend forever.

> *May God protect you and yours,*
> *Bernie*

Now that Kathy's husband had moved into his own
apartment, she and Bernie began dating openly. She
introduced him to the other nurses on her floor. Bernie
had a knack for making everyone, not just Kathy, feel
special. "Each time he came to pick me up from work,"
she now says, "he had something nice to say to the other
nurses. His age had a lot to do with it: when and how he
was raised. But it was also just him. He made you feel
like a lady."

The most feared step came next: introducing Bernie
to her children. Kathy sat them down and explained to
them she had a new friend who would be spending more
time with them. Her son, Scott, took to Bernie immediately. Bernie showed him how to pitch a fastball and
Scott proudly introduced his mom's "new friend" to the
other kids on the block. Within weeks Bernie was playing
baseball with every kid in the neighborhood. Developing
a relationship with Kathy's daughter, Kristin, would take
more time. Some days she would jump on Bernie as he

came up the walk, other days she ignored him completely. Even after Bernie and Kathy had been openly dating nearly a year, she still hadn't made up her mind on how she felt about this newcomer. When she was still five years old, Kristin pointed to Bernie at the dinner table and announced, "I don't want you to come to my first communion." Bernie was quiet, but Kathy was mortified at her daughter's behavior. She had been performing an incredible balancing act for so long between the divorce lawyers, her children, and Bernie, she lost her temper. Bernie calmed her down. He didn't have to go to the communion. It was Kristin's special day and he respected the girl's wishes. It wasn't in his gentle nature to force an issue. The day would go fine without him.

Bernie had been developing other habits even more pleasant than holding the door for Kathy or making sure he was the one to walk closest to traffic. He insisted on driving her to and from work every day. One evening, she walked into her home to find all new furniture. When her husband had moved out, Kathy told him to take whatever he wanted. Not able to afford to replace the pieces, she and the kids had been living without a couch for months. Her jaw hit the floor when Bernie opened the door for her and she saw a new living room set! One time she came home and discovered he'd varnished the baseboards around the house. On another occasion he painted a bedroom. She was stunned by Bernie's generosity. Despite the fact that her husband's job as a college administrator left his summers free, he'd never gotten around to those things. Why, it had been ages since her mother had to come over to help out with chores. "Why do you do this for me?" she asked, truly overwhelmed by his love and generosity. "Because I don't want you to worry about anything when you come home except me!" he said with a sly smile. "You think I'm being nice when really I'm being selfish." In the note at left, Bernie shows exactly how "selfish" he is.

19

When Kathy read the note, she gave Bernie a big kiss. "Gross!" Kristin, now seven, shouted. "You two are acting just like kids!" "Thank you, Kristin," Kathy said

---

KATHY'S WORK SCHEDULE

1. Walk up steps
2. Open door
3. Close door
4. Hang keys on hook
5. Hug Bernie
6. Hug Bernie
7. Do what makes you smile
8. If any questions, refer to numbers 5 and 6

I remain sincerely yours.
All my love, Bernie

from Bernie's arms. "You've just given me the best com-
pliment ever!" Her daughter was understandably con-
fused.

One evening after work, Bernie mentioned his wife
and Kathy noticed he spoke of her in the past tense.
Bewildered, Kathy asked if she was still alive. His wife
had died suddenly of a brain aneurysm some time before though he never made mention of it, not wanting
to add stress to Kathy's already hectic life. When Bernie's
son ran into financial troubles, Bernie had sold his
house and moved in with his son's family to help iron
things out. Bernie had always put the needs of everyone
else first and now she wanted to do something nice for
him. After talking with her children, she asked Bernie to
move in with her. He accepted.

It had been more than two years since she was first
charmed by Bernie's gentlemanly ways in the hospital.
With the aid of medications, including oral chemotherapy for the lymphoma, his health had remained stable.
Now that he lived with Kathy, his life was great. Since
Bernie was retired, he had plenty of time to spend with
the kids. He took them out for ice cream and to the
park. He split the responsibility of getting Kristin to basketball and piano practice, picking up Scott from chorus
and baseball. One afternoon, Kathy saw Kristin take his
hand while watching television. The little girl had come

a long way from barring Bernie from her communion. Bernie was now a part of all their lives.

Walking out of work one night, Kathy was surprised to find Bernie's sister waiting for her in the hospital parking lot. "Bernie didn't want you to worry," his sister said. He was at home with a fever. Kathy made dinner and put the kids to bed. She went to call the doctor but Bernie assured her it wasn't that serious. Later that evening, unable to sleep, he went to the couch and turned on the television. From the living room, Kathy heard a thud. She jumped out of bed to find Bernie on the floor. "Go back to sleep," he urged once he was on his feet. "Sleep?" Kathy said with alarm, "I'm calling an ambulance!"

In the intensive care unit, his body had gone into a system-wide shock. She sat by him that day, alongside Bernie's sister. "You've made him very happy," his sister told Kathy. She knew it must have been true because Bernie had made her so happy. Everyone from the kids' teachers to her neighbors to the nurses on her ward had noticed a change in Kathy over the last three years. Now that happiness was hanging from a thread. She'd never felt so helpless.

That night her son, Scott, was to perform in the choral concert. "You have to go," Bernie insisted from his hospital bed. Kathy assured him she wasn't going

21

anywhere. "If you don't go," he went on, "he'll remember it for the rest of his life. Now get out of here." Kathy rushed from the hospital to the concert, then dropped the kids off at home and went right back to Bernie's side. She hadn't found anyone to stay with the kids and couldn't stay long. In the morning, one of the nurses called her. Bernie had suffered cardiac arrest. When Kathy got to the hospital, they were applying paddles to his chest. When nothing changed she urged them to try again. And again. "Is he still in there?" she asked one of the doctors, her face streaming with tears. "Please Kathy," he told her. "Don't make me say it."

"Maybe he left you another note," Kristin said to her mom when they returned from the funeral. In the year that Bernie lived with them, he had left her mother so many nice notes around the house, perhaps there was one more. "Did you check his pockets?" the girl asked. She assured her daughter there wasn't another note except, perhaps, the love letter Bernie had written across Kathy's heart.

It used to be that getting to know one another by writing letters was a drawn-out process, one that could take months, even years. But e-mail has changed all that. Now it is possible to connect with someone else on the whim of the instant. The emotions of the moment are captured and dispatched without the second thoughts that can lead to too much caution. "Love's winged chariot" does indeed hurry near—and far—in the world of the Internet.

The Missing Piece
~~

Allison Smith's life was nearly perfect. She had a fulfilling career as an executive director for a transportation management organization, a new condo in South Florida, a plethora of friends, a caring family, a dog and a cat that she adored. The only thing missing was someone to share it all with. A stunning brunette with warm brown eyes, she had been without a significant other for nine years and was tired of it. She demanded a change.

"I was so jaded by the whole dating thing that finally I just said to AOL, 'Give me every guy who lives in Fort Lauderdale who is single and on-line *right now!*'" With that, a list of names came up.

Allison read over the profiles and was intrigued by a few. Among other things, Chad's profile described him as an airplane mechanic, an avid golfer and cyclist. "Actually," Allison remembers, "it said 'Golf, golf, and more *golf!*' I thought it was a good sign, that he was so active. And airplanes . . . that certainly sounded oh, I don't know . . . *manly*. So, I took a chance that he wasn't awful and sent him an instant message."

They made plans to meet Saturday evening since Allison had a dinner date with one of the other AOL matches on Friday. However, that fellow never showed up. "The guy canceled at the last minute and I was livid! More than that, I was really, really hungry! We were supposed to go eat." Fuming and starving, Allison was ready to run out to grab some dinner when the phone rang. It was Chad. He was calling to confirm their plans for the following evening. Still angry about her canceled date, Allison was short-tempered with Chad. Noticing she was in a bad mood, Chad asked her what was wrong. Allison was at the end of her rope with all this dating business.

"I'm just really hungry," she blurted into the phone. "Listen, if you want to just get this over with, you can come over right now." And he did. Along with roasted chicken, a salad, and mashed potatoes. From that point forward there was no looking back. Though they had exchanged pictures, it wasn't until he was standing before her that she found herself smitten with his boyish good looks and easy smile. He had a low-key demeanor when he spoke and a way of clearly explaining even the most technical aspects of his job.

It didn't take long for the Fort Lauderdale couple to begin sending romantic e-mails to each other. Looking back on the letters, Allison says, "They are pretty mushy considering some of them were written within *a week* of our meeting. Like they say, 'When you know, you just know.' And we knew!" Indeed, this first note was written a mere six days after their initial face-to-face meeting.

3/18/99

Dear Chad,

For so long, I used to lie in bed wishing I could find someone who would run his hand across my back with no ulterior motive other than to just connect with me in a loving, affectionate way. I wished for that feeling often, only to be disappointed.

Although I've had wonderful health, lots of good friends, a loving family, a good job, and two beautiful pets who have brought me a lot of joy, not having been able to find someone special to care about and share my love with has caused me to question myself. It has also been a source of deep sadness in my life . . . that is, until now.

I know it is still early in our relationship, but I am so happy that we found each other. Once, I wrote a list of all the things that were important to me in a mate. I wanted someone who was kind, affectionate, considerate, intelligent, and responsible. I wanted someone who had integrity, someone who loved animals, nature, and travel. Someone who

27
♦

cared about keeping physically fit and healthy. Someone who had his act together career-wise and financially. Of course the person had to be attractive to me . . . which usually meant he would be clean-cut with light eyes and a nice build. You are all of those things and so much more, honey.

28
◆

Chad, I care about you and promise that I will not do anything that would dishonor the relationship we have been enjoying with each other. Today, as a gesture of my feelings for you, I deleted my AOL personal ad, which had been running for nearly a year. After all, I have finally found the person who will rub my back without reservation.

> *—Love you,*
> *Allison*

The next day, Chad wrote back:

3/19/99

Allison,

Sweetheart, there is so much that I want to say to you but putting the right words together seems so hard sometimes. I want every word to be so right. I don't know if I told you how refreshing it is to have someone like you in my life. In the short time we have known each other, I have gained so much respect for you and a yearning to get to know you better. I love coming home to that beautiful smile, those gorgeous eyes, that wonderful hug, and that carefully placed kiss on my neck . . . on my lips. You have given me a reason to come home. Please know how much that statement means and the effect you have had on me. I've never thought about giving up traveling and I would give it up right now for you.

I can't wait to return home to someone so special as you! I can already feel those loving hands touching me as they do. I am going to turn in now. I am so tired but want you to know how happy I am with you and the thought of us spending a long and enjoyable life together.

—*I love you, Chad*

After countless dates, some laughable, some horrible, Allison was astonished to find so many traits about Chad she adored.

3/28/99

Chad,

It warms my heart when I think about the qualities I love and admire about you.

First of all, you are affectionate. I think I have finally met my match in that department. I love the constant touching, massaging, hugging, holding, and kissing we share. I feel so secure and loved by your affections. I know that you are loyal. I have no reason to ever doubt you.

You are easygoing. Your personality complements mine so well. You are neither picky about things nor judgmental. It doesn't matter if my grilled cheese doesn't brown or my house isn't as neat as it could be. You are always so comfortable to be around.

You are hardworking and responsible. You take your job seriously and are not deterred by your long commute and demanding schedule. You are dependable and have a good head on your shoulders. I respect you for that.

You have a soft heart for animals. I knew from the first time you let Bailey jump all over you and the first morning you got up early to put tuna in the cat's bowl. You love my "boys" as much as I do . . . as much as they love you.

You are intelligent. You know a great deal about so many things. We can talk about anything.

You are very attractive. I love when your warm hazel eyes look deep into mine, I love that great smile of yours. I love your lean body, your fabulous back and forearms, and despite what you say, I love your thighs! I cannot say enough about the softness of your skin . . . it is absolute silk! You are a very wonderful and satisfying lover and I feel like we connect well together on every level.

I love all these things about you, Chad. But what I love the most is everything you do and say makes me feel so good about

31
◆

myself. Thank you for bringing true joy into my life.

—Allison

The couple laughs at the fact that Chad basically "came over and never left!" As far as they are concerned, they have been living together since day one. However, Chad's line of work calls for him to travel across the country to repair airplanes. This, coupled with Allison's insatiable wanderlust, means the couple are often separated for weeks at a time. Once, when Chad was on assignment in Dallas while Allison was vacationing on the East African island of Madagascar, he sent this e-mail to her:

4/3/99

Hi baby. I'm sitting in my hotel room in Dallas, missing you like never before. I am falling more in love with you every day, even though you are not here. I have thought a lot about us the last few days and I have come to a conclusion: you are the perfect match for me. When you left for Madagascar, it felt as though something was taken away from me.

I woke up this morning and had the most incredible feeling. Allison, you are breaking through this barrier I had set up. You are getting to the center of my soul. You are touching the thing inside of me that makes me so very happy. I am finding myself more in love with you with each passing day.

33
◆

It's so great to have someone in your life who really appreciates the things you do, the things you say. I feel so lucky to have such a beautiful person in my life. It's such a change, to go on the road and know that when I get home I will be returning to someone who really loves me.

Sweet dreams and don't forget that little kiss you will feel once you get home.

Chad

6/2/99

Dearest Chad—My heart just soars every time I think of you. I am incredibly lucky. You have graced my life with your love. I cannot help but brag about you to everyone I know!

I am very excited about your moving in.

*Your future is my future, your success my
success, your pain my pain . . . it's so great to
travel this road called life with someone who
only wants the best for you. Yes, I am
incredibly lucky.*

34

8/8/99

    *Chad—Sweetheart, I feel so loved and
looked after and secure with you. While so
many couples are constantly arguing and
trying to work through their problems, life
with you these last five months has been so
wonderfully easy and rewarding. I'm looking
forward to our trips to Boston and up to the
Northwest, to watching Gator games and
having you join my family for Thanksgiving
and Christmas—and who knows what on the
millennium . . .*

Though Allison alluded to the possibility of a millennium wedding, she was still shaken when Chad actually asked for her hand. They had just ordered dessert at
their favorite restaurant, the French Quarter. Chad, who
had been sitting across from Allison, came around the

table to sit beside her. Allison assumed he had moved to gain easier access to the dessert they were about to share. As the two nibbled at the toasted meringue, cream, and cake of their baked Alaska, Chad put his fork down, turned to Allison, and said, "You make my life complete. I love you with all my heart. Will you marry me?"

"Unfortunately," Allison now says, "I can't remember *anything* he said after that. I was just stunned. Chad says I began to cry a lot though I don't really remember that either!" What she does remember is Chad dropping to one knee, kissing her hands, and the sound of her own voice saying yes. The couple at the table beside them offered their congratulations and noted a strange coincidence: they had become engaged at the same restaurant four months earlier. Allison and Chad became husband and wife on January 1, 2000, in the Great Smoky Mountains of Tennessee. The dawning of a new era brought to a close a solitary period in Allison's life and ushered in the *rest* of her life.

35
◆

There was a time when love letters were almost everything. They did not traverse the globe instantly, but with what seemed an agonizing slowness. During wartime the letters sent from home to a loved one in the service were mailed to a waystation, because the sender often did not know, and could not be told, where the letters were really going. And the letters that came back from "somewhere" were doubly precious, because they meant that the soldier, the sailor, the marine who had written the letter was still alive.

A Soldier's Devotion

In the stately Augusta, Maine, home of Judge Williamson, they spent the summer of 1941 working in each other's presence. He was a gardener, employed with his father's landscaping company. She looked after the Williamson children. Every now and again, their eyes would meet. "Hi, Mary Merry!" he would say, teasing her about her pretty, singsong name. She was used to it—with a name like hers, at least people would always remember her.

When Mary Merry returned to college after her summer employment at the Williamsons' home, she received a letter from the landscaper's son asking if he could correspond with her. "Yes," she wrote back to Gordon, "that would be all right." Mary was busy earning her teaching degree, however, and their correspondence was brief. Undaunted, he approached her the next year when Mary was back at the Williamsons' house. Surely, now that summer was upon them, she would have a bit of free time. He asked to take her to the pictures one evening and she shyly accepted. They saw a musical starring Fred Astaire and Ginger Rogers and then walked through town arm and arm. From that moment forward, they were a couple.

Judge Williamson's house sat high on a grassy hill. The train snaked through the valley below. From that vista, Mary saw the trains coming and going, watched as the number of boys leaving the depot in uniform rose with each passing week. All of her four brothers had already gone overseas. Her older brother George was stationed in England. One of her younger brothers was in the Philippines while the other two were fighting somewhere else in the Pacific. Often you had no idea exactly where your loved ones were.

With America's participation in World War II escalating, Gordon Oatway knew that he could be called to fight any minute. And by the end of his and Mary's blissful summer of mountain hikes and picnics, his time had come. A few weeks before he left for basic training at Fort Devon, Massachusetts, Gordon presented Mary with a gold watch. "Will you wait for me, Mary?" She said she would.

Along with Gordon's sister Betty, Mary went to see him off at the train station. Through her tears, she tried to remain upbeat, knowing the only way she could now keep his spirits high was with the ink in her pen. It would be some time before she knew exactly where he had gone. Later she would come to know that Gordon had sailed on the *Queen Mary*—which had been converted to a troopship—from New York and, by 1943, like her brother George, he was in England.

In his first letter, Gordie tried to tell her where he was stationed. But for security purposes, the name of the location had been snipped out by the army censors. Mary knew all about that problem from corresponding with her brothers. But Gordie's letter was the worst she had seen—the censor's scissors had cut across the paper so many times she couldn't make heads or tails of it. "Please write on only one side of the paper, Gordie," she wrote back to him, because each time they cut out a word, she would lose what had been written on the other side as well. It didn't take Gordon long to learn he couldn't reveal too much about his duties. Or about his deep feelings for Mary. The censors were not some anonymous board of men but a part of his outfit, and he had no intention of giving them the opportunity to tease him about the love he held for the girl back home named Mary Merry.

Unknown to Mary, Gordon worked with airplane armaments in a part of England routinely bombed by the Germans. Many of his fellow soldiers were killed or gravely wounded, but he didn't talk about that. Instead she received pleasant notes about everyday events like getting a haircut, the Ping-Pong games he'd won and lost, or a bicycle trip into town. He told her about the huge farm in Scotland they visited while on furlough, how the cows were cleaned in a separate room before getting milked with an electric milking machine. And of course, there were pranks. "The other night," he wrote to her in the fall of 1943, "I put my towel around my neck and started down to take a shower. But when I got about halfway there, I thought I had better stop in the PX and get something to eat before it closed. Warfield and two other boys knew I had gone to take a shower, so they went to the shower room and got two big pans of cold water. One of the boys looked in and there was a fellow about my size with his back facing them . . ." So while Gordon grabbed a hot meal, the other fellow had a cold shower.

Gordon returned to Maine for a week-long visit the Christmas of 1943. He had been gone for a year and Mary was thrilled to be with him again. They went to one of the nearby lakes for a day of ice fishing. As they sat by the hole cut into the ice, Gordon finally told her about the horrors he had seen, the damage caused by incendiary bombs, and the friends he had lost. She knew that he had to tell her, but it left her even more frightened for him, as well as for her brothers and herself.

The night before he left to return to Europe, Gordon slipped a ring onto Mary's finger. It was a lovely gold band with a red stone cut to look like the ruby he wanted to buy, but couldn't afford. Her answer was an enthusiastic yes. By morning he was gone.

Mary not only continued her college studies but

also took on extra volunteer work for the war effort. Along with other women in her area, she trained as a plane spotter. They learned to distinguish the silhouettes of American planes from foreign ones and sat lookout on mountaintops and fire towers. She grew a victory garden and from neighboring fields collected milkweed floss that would later be turned into stuffing for jackets and sleeping bags. When school finished for the summer, Mary picked string beans and corn at home, and then worked on a factory assembly line that manufactured mosquito bars for the boys who slept under nets in the jungles of the Pacific, and toboggans and skis for the those coping with the snows of Europe. And through it all, Mary and Gordon wrote to each other up to three times a week, although their letters sometimes arrived in a different order than they were written and sometimes took a long time to make their way across the Atlantic. Perhaps the waiting made receiving a letter all the sweeter.

43

April 24, 1944

My Dearest Mary,

> *Last evening I went for a walk alone. I could see pheasants everywhere and as I came into the end of a small field I saw eight young*

rabbits out sunning themselves. I guess the spring makes you wish you were with the one you love more than any other time. The other evening there was a dance here at the Red Cross. They bring girls from the different services up here. You had to be dressed in Class A's (good clothes) to get in and that left me out as I was too lazy to clean up.

The boys say, "Why don't you bother with the girls, Oatway? You're not married yet, there are no strings tied." I know I am old-fashioned but I plan to do the same as I would if I were married. I guess whatever you and I know about lovemaking we will have to learn while we are together. I don't know how some of the boys here who are married can do the way they do (they go all the way). Then they get pictures from home of their wife and baby and they feel like a heel, but after awhile they do the same thing over again. I am glad you and I are the way we are.

I must close now dear. Be good.

All my love,
Gordon

July 9, 1944

My Dearest Gordie,

This is a lazy summer afternoon. Not even a breeze stirs a single leaf. I can't help thinking how lovely it would be with you and a canoe on a lake, or you and a sailboat, or just you.

Everyone around here is doing their haying and the smell of the newly mown hay once in awhile floats in the open window, but even then no breeze stirs the curtain. This is just the kind of a day that's too hot to do anything in the line of work.

Do you know, honey, it was just about two years ago now that we were having the time of our lives. Remember one night (I guess it was early morning, though!) we were sitting in the Williamsons' kitchen. You were on the stool and I finally got up the courage to get near enough to put my arms around you. I said, "Gordie, I don't want you to go." Remember? Well, I meant it. When you went, it was almost like taking away my life because you already had become a part of it in the

45
•

short while that I had known you. I hated to have you go. Every hour when I was with you just flew by like a minute, and I've lived every one of those short hours over and over and over since you've been gone.

I've just been to Lewiston at the hospital to see my sister and her new little boy. I just couldn't help envying her, Gordie. She has two little boys and they're the sweetest things anyone could ever dream for. I hope we can have children someday not too far away. And I want my boys to be like their dad. Boys that will grow up to be men with a good level head on two firm shoulders. I can't think of anything that could be more wonderful than to have you and a little home that we could call our own and to know that you were home and safe and would be there always and always.

I do really love you and I know I always will. Gordie, I've been good all the time you've been gone and I will be till you come back to me.

Goodnight, Mary

There had been nothing to prevent Mary and Gordon from marrying when he came home for Christmas in 1943. But instead, they just got engaged. When so many couples were rushing to the altar during the war, why didn't they do the same? "We hadn't known each other long enough," Mary says now. "Besides, it gave us both something to look forward to."

June 22, 1944

My Dearest Mary,

Mother keeps telling me in her letters that she has read how the army is changing so many of the boys for the worse and she is worrying for fear it will change me. As long as I have someone like you to work for I could never change for the worse. I get pretty discouraged at times, but I always get over it. I was telling one of the boys tonight that I always hoped I could find a girl who had lived as clean a life as I, but I found one who was better than I. If you weren't the most understanding girl in the world you would have told me where to go before this.

It seems as if the time will never come

when I can get home to you, but it won't be so long now, I hope.

If you find a picture in this letter it will be of me after one of our hunting expeditions. I guess I look like a tramp, but those are the clothes we work in. I have a rabbit in one hand and a slingshot in the other.

All my love, I am always thinking of you.

Gordon

P.S. I am sorry dear, but I can't send that picture in this letter. I will send it soon.

Mary became more worried as the American and British forces moved forward across Europe in the winter of 1945. The newspapers made it clear that the Germans were fighting fiercely to hold every inch of ground. It had been nearly fourteen months since she had seen Gordie or heard his voice. Often, as she wrote him, she found herself feeling his ring on her finger. And now it had been weeks since she had heard anything back from him at all.

February 23, 1945

My Dearest Gordie,

Days go by and still no word. I just keep on wondering. Honey, are you all right? Those last letters are getting very thin and worn.

Honey, you asked me in a letter awhile ago if I would like to live in the city or in the country. If we had a nice little home in the country, I'd love it. I never want to live right in town or a city unless I have to. I like the good wholesome country. I can just picture a nice little house with some good neighbors quite near to ask in once in a while.

What I want most is you. A house and the country and everything are essentials but you are the core of it all.

I'd like to be in your pocket now and see what you're doing and know you're safe.

Dot and I were asked over to South Paris on Sunday to go skiing with the owner of the Paris Manufacturing Co. where we worked last summer making skis and toboggans for the army. We planned to have

49
•

*an outdoor dinner and ski all day, but with
the way it's been raining, I wonder if we
can go. Maybe later we can go to Mt.
Washington. There is still snow there until
June.*

*Sometime you and I will climb Mt.
Washington together. It is a wonderful feeling,
but you have to experience it to know.*

*I'd climb every mountain from here to
there if I could find you.*

God bless you wherever you are,

Mary

A phone call a few days later from Gordon's mother
saved Mary from guessing at the whereabouts of her
fiancé any longer. He was on his way home. His mother
had received a call saying he was back at Fort Devon and
was due to arrive in Maine the next day. Mary, now a
teacher at a school forty miles outside of Augusta,
arranged to have a substitute and jumped on the morning bus. She went straight over to the Oatway house
from the terminal, her heart racing with delight. Mary
was so happy to see Gordon safe and in one piece that
she showered him with hugs and kisses without a

thought about his parents, who were standing there in the living room watching them.

Mary and Gordon finally married June 23, 1946. Many people would always remember her as Mary Merry, but she happily gave up her singsong name under an arch of orange blossoms and blue spruce to become Mrs. Gordon Oatway.

Young love is rich with promises as well as passion. The wide future lies ahead, and while no one can know what it will hold, that doesn't keep anyone from dreaming. Letters in which those dreams are set down hold a special place in the annals of love—their ardent words renew the hopes of us all. Oh yes, we say, let's go, let's set forth again, if only for a moment, on that fresh path to the world that might someday be.

Let's Go—I'm with You

They were just out of high school and neither of them had a lot of money. Still, James wanted to take his girlfriend Beth to a nice meal. He was leaving for Fort Louis in a few days for ROTC training. He wanted to leave her with a memory that would last the six weeks he would be gone: dinner at Joe Federico's, the one restaurant they'd always wanted to try. It wasn't the fanciest place in the world—families, local merchants, even the college kids from the nearby University of Oregon went there on special occasions—but for them, it might as well have been an evening at the Ritz.

Joe Federico's is divided into two sections: the upstairs is reserved for fine dining while the downstairs is more casual, less expensive. With the budget of teenagers, of course they would be dining downstairs. James knew that his girl deserved the best though it wasn't in his reach. A few weeks into his training at Fort Louis, he sent Beth this letter.

My Beth,

I think about you constantly. Yeah, I think about making love to you—how much I miss being part of you, having that connection to you. It's so basic and beautiful. So natural. I miss being able to hold you when I need you. But I have you in my heart and between my ears so you're here when I need comfort.

56

When I'm feeling down, I just concentrate on a memory of us and my mood jumps right back up again. I hold the envelope with your perfume. One deep inhalation and suddenly the world has edges again, it's no longer faded or blurred. Suddenly, everything has a reason again. The smell of your perfume floods a vision of you into my mind. You pour out of my mind to soothe me, to run your hands over my face and lift my chin. You kiss my forehead, take my hands and hold me against you very quietly until all the pain and depression disappears. Then life has color again. I bury my face in your hair and kiss that spot just below your ear and you smile and flare your eyes at me, scolding me. I tickle you and you squeal and roll away, grab me and jump on top of me, try to hold me down. But I kiss you

*instead and your will to fight softens in my
arms. And when I say I love you, you answer,
"Good!" Then I frisk you for being smart. You
let your guard down and reply, "I love you,
James Stegall."*

*Oh, man. Then the world is fireworks
and neon, a billion people dancing crazy in
the streets. Beth loves me! I'll light the moon
on fire, play pinball with planets, run around
the earth, smash mountains singing like a
fool. I'll roll in green fields grabbing daisies for
you just to see you smile. I'll tear down the
night to make you an evening dress—skin
tight, flashed with diamond star sequins and
we'll strut across the sky on our way to Joe
Federico's and this time we'll go upstairs!
We'll walk through on a green carpet of
hundred dollar bills so the waiters will fight
for the chance to refill your coffee. Your hair
will be like the sun against your nightdress
and your smile will make the universe rotate
in rhythm. You can have as many oyster
shooters as you can suck down and wine is
like complimentary water. A hundred bottles?*

57
◆

Why not? Afterward, we'll go to the top of
Skinner's Butte Park and watch the city lights
spread out the black velvet hills, flashing and
twinkling like a carnival of grins, gliding
Ferris wheels and charging roller coasters.
That's life, that's ours, honey. Hold my hand.
  Let's go.

                    James

Letters written from far away during a period of necessary separation become a kind of lifeline, a way of making sure that hearts remain tethered to each other. Reassurance may be the most prevalent theme, but there can be surprises too. One may even discover that one has been loved even before one knew it.

In Love and at War

On the morning of December 30, 1941, Dorothy's father left for work and her mother went into town for shopping. As far as they knew, their daughter was going to her job at Mallory's Jewelry Store in Monongahela, Pennsylvania. But Dorothy Douglas had other plans. She left a note for her mother and left the house wearing three dresses, one on top of the other—not because of the December cold but because she knew it might be some time before she would be allowed in her family's home again. Dorothy eloped that day with Albert Dunkerton, whom Dorothy and everyone else called Dunk. She was nineteen years old, and she knew that Dunk was the man for her, whatever her parents might think.

They had met when his friend Bud Kinder, who didn't have a car, convinced Dunk into going on a double date. Bud was dating Martha, Dorothy's best friend, and Dunk did have a car—a perfect setup, so far as Bud could see. Dunk agreed to help his friend out, and was astonished to discover that Dorothy was the girl who used to work in the candy store he went to. He had gone to that store several times just to look at Dorothy, just to hear her charming voice and feel her slender fingers touch his when he handed her a few cents for a piece of licorice. Now there she was, just like a fairy princess, in a red velvet dress puffed at the sleeves and swinging out from her waist.

The two couples drove around that snowy night, then stopped in a drugstore for a Coke. Dorothy and Dunk were getting along better than Martha and Bud ever would! Neither Dorothy nor Dunk were into dancing or living the high-life. They talked about books, movies, and plays until it was time for the girls to go home. That night, Dunk walked Dorothy to her door and gave her a kiss goodnight. It only took that one evening. Both knew they were destined to be together forever.

A few days later, Dorothy introduced Dunk to her mother and father. It was a polite meeting though Mrs. Douglas had a funny wrinkle in her brow the entire time. It was as if she were trying to work out a jigsaw puzzle or crossword. It wasn't Dorothy she was worried about. The Douglases kept a keen eye on their daughter. Sure, they were stricter with her than they had ever been with their sons but, they often reminded Dorothy, that's just the way it was. Dorothy had been a good student in high school. She attended church and even taught Sunday school. She'd worked at the candy store and now at the jewelry shop, always contributing part of her wages to the family. It was this young man Mrs. Douglas wasn't too sure about. But she couldn't figure out why.

"Albert, does your mother belong to Eastern Star?" Dorothy's mother asked, naming just one of the many social clubs where she was a member. When Dunk said no, she ran down a list of other local ladies' auxiliaries. "The Mothers Club? Kiwanis?" He answered no to every organization she named. So why did his last name sound so familiar?

63
•

The young couple left for the evening, Mrs. Douglas reminding Dorothy of her curfew. Finally, it hit Mrs. Douglas like a bolt of lightning. Of course Mrs. Dunkerton didn't belong to any ladies' clubs! With a reputation like hers, who could call her a "lady"? Not that Dorothy's mom had ever *met* Albert's mother or even knew if the rumors were true. Gospel or gossip, it didn't matter: Dorothy was forbidden to see Albert Dunkerton ever again. She argued and cried and tried to remind them that Dunk was an honest young man with a good job as a blacksmith. Her parents wouldn't listen, and she began to act like a different girl. She would sneak behind her parents' backs, catching a few precious moments with her beau whenever she could. She would tell little lies to hide her whereabouts. When Dunk could not be near her, he wrote her love notes. Dunk would give the notes to one of her girlfriends to deliver to Dorothy. Once a letter made it to her, she inhaled every delicious word before stuffing it in a bathing cap with all the others. She placed the cap securely behind her desk. One afternoon, she returned from work to find her parents sitting at the kitchen table, her letters from Dunk spread across the table like a deck of playing cards. Dorothy was humiliated. They had read every single one, and that night they forced her to watch as they burned the letters.

"I was a good girl!" Dorothy says now, her voice still registering the injustices from so long ago. "But they treated me like a criminal."

Around that time, Dorothy was hospitalized with appendicitis. In the Douglas family, it was not a condition to be taken lightly. One of Dorothy's brothers had died from that very ailment just the year before when he was only fifteen. It was a serious situation that required immediate surgery. Surely, her parents would allow Dunk a hospital visit. He knocked on Dorothy's hospital door only to be thrown out of the room by her father. Dunk was sick with worry. Every night Dorothy was in the hospital, Dunk quietly parked his car outside her window then flashed the lights a few times. Dorothy, who couldn't get out of her bed and walk to the window, angled her compact mirror until Dunk came into view. She would fall asleep looking at the reflection of the man who loved her, sitting in his car in the parking lot.

Dorothy recovered from the surgery and, having been scared that she'd never see Dunk again, they began to think about eloping. Everyone was getting engaged and now Dorothy was, too. "Here's mine," one of Dorothy's coworkers at the jewelry store chimed, thrusting out her hand showing off the large diamond set in gold. "Well, here's mine," the other salesgirl said, splaying her fingers so all could get a gander at the blinding stone set in her ring. "Yes," Dorothy joined in, so eager to be part of the club even if she did have to take the ring off once she got home, "here's mine!" Her two coworkers squinted their eyes and slowly leaned toward Dorothy's outstretched hand as if examining a dead bug. It was a tiny, chipped diamond on a simple gold band. "You're kidding," one of the girls said with disbelief, turning to Dorothy with pity in her eyes. Dorothy proudly admired the $7 engagement ring on her finger. She couldn't care less what it had cost. It signified a love of irreplaceable value to her.

Their elopment caused the expected rift with Dorothy's family, but the following spring the family was reunited when Dorothy's mother was also struck by appendicitis and Dunk took Dorothy to the hospital to see her. In time the Douglases were able to see in Dunk the same wonderful qualities that Dorothy had recognized from the start. By 1943, the Dunkertons had been blessed with a baby boy. Not long after, Dunk was called to duty in the war. They had gone through so much just to be together and now they were about to be torn apart. Both tried to remain upbeat as Dunk prepared to leave but it was impossible. They wept in each other's arms as he waited to board the train to Camp Peary Naval base for training. There he got lucky. Because of his high test scores in English, Dunk was assigned to sailors who didn't know how to read or write. He also put his language skills to use in letters to Dorothy.

April 14, 1944

My Own Dearest One,

> *Darling, before I start this, let me tell you that I mean every word of this. Every line I write will be exactly as my heart dictates it to me. My sweet, I didn't start to live until the night I met you. You knew we were meant for each other right then, didn't you? I felt as though I had known you all my life. Remember how we talked as if we knew we were going to be together forever?*

> *I'll always remember the starlight in your eyes the first time that I kissed you, when you said that you were mine. It took my heart*

*away for good. That first kiss was the one I'd
waited for all my life.*

*Sweetheart, you have done wonders with
me. Sometimes I think if I had not had a
wonderful woman like you I might not have
made as much of my life as I have. Every
effort I put forth is for you. You have made
quite a change in me.*

67
•

*Darling, there is no one in this world who
could ever mean as much to me as you do.
You are all my life. I'll always remember every
single tear you shed for me. Each one was a
drop of blood from my heart. When I left for
the service and you cried, it made me feel
miserable. It was all I could do to keep myself
under control. If I were to let myself go, I
would have cried more than you did.*

*I'm waiting for the day when I can come
home to you and take my place in your heart
where I belong. Maybe then I could be more of
a companion, husband, and lover to you than
I was before.*

*I still think of you as my sweetheart and
I'm afraid I always shall. No, I don't mean*

*you haven't been a good wife for I could never
have one better, but I feel more as a lover
toward you than a husband. A husband and
wife I don't think could be quite the same or
as happy as we are.*

68

*I close my eyes and I can see you just as you
looked last time I saw you—smiling and stomp-
ing up and down, waving good-bye. I wish you
were doing that now . . . except waving hello.*

Dunk

While he was stationed in Virginia, Dorothy was sad but
at least she knew he was safe teaching the sailors. That
sense of reassurance crumbled when he was called to
active duty. Since he'd been a blacksmith before the war,
they both figured he would be working as a fitter on a
ship. But neither of them knew for sure.

1944—Treasure Island, California

My Darling Wife,

*Tonight my heart is breaking. I had to do
something that I have dreaded to do since I
left last March. To call you and tell you good-*

bye. I knew this moment was coming but I could never quite bring myself to believe it. My sweetheart, I'm so nervous and choked up I don't know what to do.

Keep yourself and our son well, honey. I didn't cry tonight until I told you that I love him and you so much. Honey, I can't write anymore. I can't even see the paper.

. . . I feel a little better now. I took out the pictures you gave me and set them up here. You two look so sweet. I just kissed you both.

I don't know where I am going or why. As I said, probably some island we have taken. Must be for work for we received very little gear: shoes, canteen, mosquito net, raincoat and a mess kit. No knife or anything. That is why I think it is a work detail.

Don't worry about me too much. I will be careful as I can. I love my family too much to be careless or foolish.

It was wonderful to talk to you my dearest. You really do love me, don't you? I am so happy that we have our son. I love him as much as I love you and know you will

69
•

always have a part of me beside you no matter what.

I didn't sleep much last night. I had too much on my mind. I fretted, lying there thinking of everything we had ever said and done. They can take everything else from me but never that.

70

It hurt me to make you cry. That is one thing that really makes me feel miserable. It tears my heart out. I told the chaplain. He said he knew how I felt. I have much to say and don't know how. All I can think is "I'm leaving them . . . when will I see them again?" I belong to you body and soul. I always did and I always will. You will be in my mind asleep or awake. If you only knew how I yearn to hold you in my arms and kiss you and tell you of my deep love for the most wonderful wife a man could ever have.

Love, Dunk

Along with the unmentionable dread of a submarine's torpedo finding his ship, Dunk feared for the worst at home as well. He'd left a one-year-old son behind and couldn't help but be concerned that the boy had a father he barely knew. He wasn't one for the party lifestyle; he was a family man and his family was half a world away. Anytime sadness or fear overwhelmed him, Dunk would take out a picture of Dorothy holding Douglas in her lap. Just looking at his family back home gave him focus. It was for them that he was fighting this awful war. Often he would find himself daydreaming about the future; of having another child, a little girl who looked like her mommy. Other times, his thoughts wandered to the past. In the letter below, he replays the night of their first meeting, reveling in each detail.

1945

> *As I sat at my lonely mid-watch tonight,*
> *my mind wandered over a myriad of small*
> *unrelated things, yet fitting so snugly into the*
> *pattern of our lives. I mentally thumbed*
> *through my book of memories and laughed at*
> *the funny and happy pages and sobered at the*
> *less enjoyable ones. I recalled how Bud called*
> *and asked me to go out on a double date. I*
> *went, not the least bit interested and expected*
> *to find a nice, solemn toothache for a date.*
> *And what did it turn out to be but an angel, a*

lovely angel, in a red velvet dress. Before we
both knew it, we were talking as if we had
known each other always and would always
remain together.

Dorothy had long since given up her job at the jewelry store. She now spent her days with her son and, every now and then, an evening with her girlfriends. Some nights, they would try to guess exactly where their husbands were. They could guess all night long, but it was always a mystery. Dunk, of course, wasn't allowed to reveal his exact location. Yet, he did decide to let Dorothy in on one secret he'd been keeping.

April 4, 1945

Hello Sweetheart,

Oh, for a nice soft bed with deep springs
and a mattress! I slept the last four nights on
a bare canvas bunk. It is good for stiffening
the back, but gosh. Everyone has left for their
ships except myself and four other guys so we
have better access to the facilities now. I
figure I'll get tomorrow off. I spent another
day in the bilge today painting and, after

*showering, shaving, and a change of clothes,
I feel swell.*

*We had some grand pineapple pie and ice
cream for chow at noon. I weighed myself
today: 198 lb. Now, if I can only harden that
up I will be a trim job for my honey! Gee, it
will be quite a time when I get back. I will
have to learn how to act and be very careful
with my speech as I have picked up a terrible
habit of the use of profane language. If you
could hear me most certainly you would be
shocked and your mother, she would have a fit.*

*It has just started to drizzle slightly and I
enjoy it for it cools the ship off a little,
although it isn't so terribly warm here. In fact,
I would venture to say it is just comfortable
for lounging about.*

*Are you still saving your love for me? I
know you are and I shall be around to collect
it just as soon as Uncle Sammy permits. I
think I'll tell you something I never told you.
Did you know I used to come in and buy
candy from you regularly? I used to think,
"Gee, I wish I had a girl like her." Then I*

*would think, "Naw, I'm not good enough for
someone like her . . . I'm only a bum and she
is so swell and elegant." I still feel the same
way. You're too good for a booby like me!*

Dorothy was shocked beyond belief. They'd been married over three years and he never once mentioned that he remembered her from the candy store! After she read the letter, she thought about all they'd been through: sneaking love letters, her parents' disapproval, eloping. And now it turned out that Dunk had not only been her best friend and lover, but her secret admirer, too.

Even though he was busy in the Pacific, Dunk never tired of making gifts for his wife. He carved her animal figurines from peach pits and even made her a silver bracelet from Australian coins. She cherished each gift just as she had cherished her engagement ring.

When Dunk was discharged in New York, he called his wife from the naval base ecstatic to be so near to home. Dorothy immediately began talking about getting a sitter and coming to the train station to meet him. To her surprise, Dunk didn't want her to come down. He wanted to walk up the stairs of their home, use the keys he'd been carrying around for months, and scoop his wife and his son up in his arms. "I want to come to you," he said. "I want to come home."

As the day broke, Dunk did walk up the stairs and straight into the heaven of his wife's arms, just as he wanted. Despite all Dunk's fears, young Douglas took to his father right away and in time, their little girl, Leslie, was born. She was just the red-haired, green-eyed daughter he'd spent so many hours on shipboard daydreaming about!

Dunk returned to work as an iron worker while building a dream home of cedar and stone for his now complete family. Dorothy continued to raise the kids and began training horses, a career she maintained for over thirty years. As the children got older, Dorothy and Dunk always maintained an open mind when it came to meeting friends the kids brought home. They refused to repeat the mistakes of Dorothy's parents, whose actions forced their daughter to run off wearing three dresses one chilly December morning.

Sometimes people have a hard time believing their own good luck. She loves me? Can that be possible? He loves me? How did that happen? When one feels like that, a letter can be a way of convincing oneself that wonderful things are really happening. Such letters can be a way of pinching oneself to make sure it isn't all a dream.

Surrendering Your Heart

They had seen each other so many times before. They'd passed one another around campus; they'd run into each other at parties. Then Peter's roommate began dating Heather's roommate. Yet it wasn't until an end-of-the-year party that they spent time alone. They got to talking, then removed themselves from the crowded room, from the loud music and cigarette smoke. They wandered outside into the warm southern California evening. Sitting on the lawn, away from the racket and chaos of college revelers, they kept talking and talking and . . . what had come over Heather? She had always been such a protective person. She was used to leading a stressful life and had never felt the need to burden any-one else with her problems. Why was she telling this person, practically a stranger, everything. *And*, she had to wonder, *why wasn't he running away?*

Peter listened to all she had to say, offering a word of encouragement here and a little advice there, though he was careful not to sound condescending or pitying. Something told him the last thing this woman needed was pity. He let her talk all night long until they found themselves contained in each other's arms, kissing, whispering. Was that a tear he felt through his shirt? Heather was exhausted from a life of keeping secrets, from always having to be strong and fighting for everything she had. She had found a confidante in the most unexpected person, in the most unexpected place—and he was leaving the next evening to spend the summer at home. They cherished their intoxicating moments together that night and for part of the next day, and then he was gone to a city three hours away.

8/7/96

Dear Heather,

You have sunk your teeth into my mind. The time we spent together was perfect. I feel as though I'm drunk, that's how happy you've made me. How dare you! It's not that I've never been happy before, but you make me feel different. I don't know how to explain it. If you decided that you didn't like me, I'd be crushed but I would be happy to know what it felt like for one night to forget the world and concentrate only on one person. To feel your body next to mine, to feel your soul, to feel your thoughts. I really never thought I would know any of these things.

So many times I have felt unlovable. You take all those destructive emotions away from me. You snatch them away and turn them into memories. I just want to go out with you and never come home. We could have millions of adventures. I would love to run away with you. So if I ever decide to run away, will you come with me?

81
♦

Is it possible to fall in love with someone in one night? Reading the letters of Peter and Heather, it seems as though they knew what was happening, yet couldn't quite comprehend it or give it a name. A few weeks after their initial meeting, Heather drove to visit Peter in his hometown, and their feelings became even more intense. In the letter below, Heather also dances around the subject of love, seductively posing the question, "Is it love when you can taste another person's soul?"

8/11/96

Dear Peter,

It's so hot here. Walking home from school was like trekking through some of the warmer, more uncomfortable sections of hell.

Sitting here now in air-conditioning without you here somehow seems infinitely worse—worse than hell, worse than heat, worse than being at school. I can't believe how fast I've gone from attraction to obsession—what is it about you that so captivates me, commands my attention, seduces my whole being? It must be everything. You are everything.

82

Now when I think about you, I can't comprehend how I didn't see all of this before. I guess it just wasn't our time—planetary alignment, solar eclipse, earthquakes, statues that cry real tears, and you and I entwined on the futon oblivious to it all. You seem to instinctively know how to kill me with pleasure, but I suspect this is because we are so very much alike in our desire. When I kiss you it's so much deeper and so much more meaningful than anything else I've yet to experience. Is that love? Is it love when you can taste another person's soul? I don't know what love is, but I certainly feel it's close—closer now with your warm breath grazing my throat or your clever lips upon my awkward mouth.

I feel the words curling on my tongue over and over but I'm afraid of them. You're near me and I feel the words circling inside my mouth, but I swallow them. I'm poisoning myself with denied confessions and repressed declarations. So, you say you are frightened? Good! You should be.

I am.

I was beginning to believe I would never find the right person. It's not that I'm desperate—lots of guys have asked me out, but they are simply unacceptable. I'm a secretive, somewhat guarded person and I can't allow just any idiot to come barging into my life with assumptions and intentions. I've always thought the person that I let in would have to have "a certain something," otherwise it would be like breeding with another species. You are so much of that "certain something" that I don't even possess a means to measure it.

Thank you for sharing your beautiful self with me,

Heather

What unfolded that night of the party? What had they whispered in the dark? Though Heather was seen by many as outgoing and bold, inside she had always felt alone in the world. Her parents divorced after only a few years of marriage and Heather's father, when he was around, was prone to heavy bouts of depression. Her mother began hearing voices when Heather was in grade school and was soon diagnosed with schizophrenia. The different medications she took made it hard for her to look after her daughter. From then on Heather had lived with her grandmother, a woman who never thought she'd be raising children well into her golden years. Neither schoolmates nor neighbors knew what her life was really like, that her mother was ill, that her father was unreliable. Yet it was a heaviness she dragged with her wherever she went.

When Heather's dad was feeling good, he could be a generous man. Father and daughter would take trips up the California coast, would make surprise visits to relatives or amusement parks. When he was low, he was absent, sometimes for days, sometimes for years. Every time he came and went, Heather's personal sense of stability shook as though she were experiencing an earthquake. Then, in 1993, no longer able to see the positive at all, her father took his life. Heather told no one. It was *her* father who'd died, no one else's. She felt if she

84
•

allowed herself to get sad, if she started thinking like either of her parents, then she would end up like them. So Heather dealt with the pain just as she dealt with everything else. With strength and secrecy.

A year later, she entered college. There, Heather was determined to make more friends, to reach out. Once classes started it seemed as if everything was going according to plan. She was making friends, going to parties, doing well in her studies. Once again, it was her strength that kept her afloat. Then, just over a year after her father passed away, Heather got a call from her grandmother. There had been a complication with one of the new medications her mother was prescribed. An experimental drug that had yet to go through full government testing had caused her system to shut down. "She's on life-support," her grandmother said.

At the hospital, they assumed Heather was underage when in actuality she was nineteen. "It was a really good thing I didn't have to make that decision," she says. "I don't know if I could have handled that." It was Heather's grandmother who made the decision to take Heather's mother off life-support the next day.

Heather cannot pinpoint why she chose the night of that party, why she chose Peter, to open her heart to. But she did. And he listened. He didn't run away. He told her about his own fears of being in a relationship,

85

fears of falling in love and being hurt. He held her on the lawn outside the party, the stars above them the only witnesses to a feeling growing between them that neither could quite dare to name.

8/15/96

86
◆

Peter, Peter, the Anteater . . .

Drinking Coke out of a large fluted champagne glass and thinking of you . . . although I must admit I wish I had you instead of the thought of you, Diet Coke instead of regular and clean dishes.

It seems the longer I know you the more I grow to truly admire you. Forgive me if I seem egotistical or self-obsessed, but I feel I deserve love in large beautiful quantities. I think I deserve it more than most people because I've lived with far less of it than most people. Sometimes this has been my fault, me not allowing others to love me. Often it has been the cruelty of several circumstances.

My whole life I dreamed of belonging somewhere and of having people who don't

mix their kindness with such large doses of
cruelty and criticism. Up until this last year,
I've been a stranger. As I told you before, my
mother was very ill and was too preoccupied
with her own loneliness. I hated her for
cheating me and not giving me what it
seemed like everyone else had: safety, stability,
normalcy, affection, understanding. I spent
my childhood mostly playing alone, inventing
and dreaming different lives for myself. With
other children, I was desperate, always trying
to get attention. "Heather talks too much, is
disruptive, and won't allow the other children
to do their work." How many times have I
seen that written on report cards?

Sometimes I feel like I pretty much raised
myself, ignoring my family and their methods.
My dad disappeared periodically for years at a
time, coming back from trips with presents
and humor and not much else. I saw him often
some years, but he was more like a distant
friend. He was not a father. I guess that's why I
was able to handle the loss so well. I love my
parents as people, but don't feel like I ever had

a parent. I didn't have any siblings. I have my grandmother, but she's always given me more pain than anything else. She and my aunt taught me self-hate by word and example. They were always quick to point out how much they had given me, how I'd never gone without anything. The things they talked about were always materialistic. Honestly, I played as easily with rocks and cardboard boxes as I did with those fifty cold Barbie dolls. I would have rather been in a normal family that was calm and simple and rational.

I feel my experience is twice that of my years. My life has been so much heartbreak and betrayal that now, I want only good things . . . it must be close to my time. It must be my turn for some happiness that is real and not something I invented in my head, pretending it was true. I am very strong and know my life will be extraordinary. I don't doubt that, but I hope it can be in an increasingly positive way. I'm glad I've become a part of your life. I will never hurt you. And if I do, know that I'm very good at being sorry.

These feelings are so wonderful and

*strange to me that I want to make every little
moment last long enough to create memories
that will sustain me. I am a passionate person
and the essence of that is the ability to savor
things, to wring every last drop of pleasure
from the moment. Very small, insignificant
things become important and enticing. Big
things become overwhelming and so beautiful
that they are barely endurable. I have never
shared such a spiritual and strange kiss as
yours. I swear for an instant I felt us overlap.
You amaze me and I want to let you in. I
want to show you the pieces of myself I've
never shown anyone, but I don't want you to
be afraid or look away or offer your sympathy
or judge me wrongly. I keep replaying the
night we met over and over in my head. I can
still feel your eyelashes brushing against my
cheek and your fingers in my hair. My heart
hasn't slowed from the intense rhythm it
adopted that night. If I didn't feel so good, I'd
say I was ill. Hmmm . . . lovesick? Must be so.*

89
♦

*Perpetually yours,
Heather*

8/18/96

Heather,

*You know what you make me feel like?
You know those freezing cold mornings and
you can feel the chill on your face, but your
body is so soft and warm. So you put your
head underneath the covers so your entire
body can feel that way and then you feel like
you just want to melt into the sheets and stay
there forever. That's how I feel with you.*

But that's only part of it.

*The truth is you scare me. It's true. See,
you seem to be so experienced and you know
what you're doing. And me, on the other
hand—I feel like I'm in a huge dark room full
of furniture and I'm trying to find my way
around. But you help me. You're in the room
with me and you have a slight glow. You don't
illuminate very much of the room, just
enough for me to see in silhouettes. I think
you could shine so bright and fill the room.
And I still find it hard to believe you're in the
room with me. It's just because I'm so used to*

being in there alone. Sometimes I smile in the
dark. You can't see me, but I know that you
know I'm smiling. And you know it's because
of you. Sometimes I close my eyes and block
your light from my sight, to see if I can
remember what it was like before you came
along.

91
•

Peter no longer has to feel as though he is in the
dark. Once they were able to become vulnerable to each
other, there was no choice but to let love in. Four years
later, Peter and Heather married to the graceful sounds
of fingertips brushing against a harp and ocean waves
crashing beyond.

A letter of apology must always be sincere if it is to be truly accepted. There are times when such a letter keeps on giving, over so many years that the sender and the recipient, to their mutual amusement, have forgotten crucial details about what made the apology necessary in the first place. But there can also be an awareness that it was very important, back then, for the apology to be made. If it had not been, who knows what might have happened?

Staying True

It was a mistake neither Chris nor Tom Ellison can recall with any amount of clarity. "Just from reading the letter, we know it was, shall we say, 'an indiscretion,'" Chris says with an easy laugh from her home in Escondido, California, "but for the life of us, we can't remember who it was with!" The Ellisons can joke about it now, but in 1968, one would have thought it was the end of the world for eighteen-year-old Tom. The strapping athlete with hazel eyes and "dimples that wouldn't stop" had gone on a date with another girl.

Tom Ellison had a reputation around the campus as a ladies' man. Indeed, when Chris Van Volkinburg first moved to the rural community of Trumansburg, New York, Tom already had a girlfriend. Sixteen-year-old Chris, the exotic "new girl in town," also began dating. Her ill-fated relationship, however, would soon end by way of the best ammunition teenagers have: humiliation. "I had been dating a boy," she recalls, "and Tom was dating another girl, but I had heard through the grapevine that he liked me. It's a small town and Tom had lots of cousins we went to school with. So one day, while I was in my English class, his cousins grabbed my boyfriend in the hall. They waited until the lesson started and shoved the poor guy through the door! My whole English class stared at him, stared at me, then burst out laughing. He was so embarrassed and I was just mortified. That was Tom's cousins' way of letting me know it was over for me and that boy—that Tom liked me."

Once Chris and Tom became a couple, things got serious quickly. Tom even went so far as to propose marriage to her while they stood in the cafeteria lunch line. But he nearly lost Chris when he made the mistake of asking the now-forgotten girl for a date. It was one of Chris's sisters who told her what Tom had done. Angry and hurt, Chris was ready to break it off. Here is Tom's earnest plea for forgiveness, written in the moody, desperate language of a teenager in love.

2:30 A.M.

Dearest Chris,

Well, there really isn't too much I can say and maybe the less said the better for both of us. I'm saying I'm sorry even though I have no right to really say it. Even though, my darling, I'm truly sorry. No matter how many girls I take out, there will be no girl that I love more than you. That's coming from my heart and

not my foolish and crippling emotions. So the
hell *with any other girl that I shall see! Your*
face, with its own little beauty and charm, will
linger and haunt me for life and I shall never,
never forget it. I love you, I like you, and I
want to eventually marry you, even though
I'm really destroying my chances with you.
Chris, if I could only say the right words or do
the right things to make you happy and to
make you always love me. I pray to God that
we were meant for each other, 'cause I've
never, nor will I ever again, love a girl as much
as I love you. I just hope you can love me. No, I
guess I can't ask that of you since it's asking too
much for a girl that has been hurt as bad as
you have. Try not to give up hope with me. I'll
never give up hope that we'll get together. I'm
not as bad as it seems sometimes, truly. I love
you *(only) and* always *will!*

97

Whether it be winter, spring, summer, or fall
or whether it rain, shine, or snow
I'll always enjoy them all
for there is one thing I must know.

Where, oh where is love?
Does it shine from the sky above?
Only the birds that once flew
will know that love is what I hold so very
dear for you.

[Here, Tom draws a heart with his name written
inside then writes:]

Have my heart, I'll have no use for it till
we get together again. It means very little to
me now. Someday it'll mean my whole life
(with you).

Love always and
never-ending, Tom
Good-nite my
darling.

P.S. You can shut me out of your life
completely, but never again will something like
this happen, and I'm going to chase after you
to the ends of the earth if I have to. I love you,
that's why! I know you know deep down inside
your heart I do. I'll never hurt you again if I
ever get another chance with you.

Tom gave the letter to Chris. After she had read it, he asked if he could take her for a drive, and she consented. They parked on a quiet road and, as they sat in his light green Chevy Impala, Tom promised to never hurt her again. Then, Chris recounts, the strangest thing happened. "The tears started to flow," she says. She had never seen Tom cry. "Here was this boy, a basketball player, a football star, the high school hunk: crying. I think it really scared him, what he was feeling for me. Our relationship was more serious than he realized."

In 1971, Chris and Tom married.

99
•

There are times when people resist love, not because they dislike the person offering that love, but because they are afraid to respond. They may simply not be ready yet for such deep feelings, or they may have suffered in the past from being too trusting. At such times, letters may be the best way to break through the defenses of someone who both does and does not want to be loved again.

Breaking Down Barriers

Just as Jennifer was walking out the door for lunch, the telephone rang. It was a client she'd been trying to get hold of all day and she had to take the call. When she hung up the phone she was surprised to find her friend Jason standing at her desk, frozen in wide-eyed silence. She had known him for a very long time; they had even been sweethearts in high school. Recently they had met up again, but they were just friends. "You're not supposed to be here," Jason stammered. "The phone . . ." she tried to explain but found it hard to finish her thought when she saw the bouquet of flowers in his hand. It wasn't her birthday, she hadn't been sick, there was no reason for him to bring her flowers unless . . . her face turned red.

Jason, knowing Jennifer took her lunch at the same time every day, had wanted her to find the bouquet when he was far from her office. Now that was impossible. He handed her the flowers and an envelope, offering no explanation for either. "You want to come over for dinner on Thanksgiving?" he asked casually, as if the situation was completely normal. "Yes," she nodded, "that sounds good." Jason mumbled an awkward good-bye and made his way out of the building. Jennifer looked at the flowers and the envelope in her hands, unsure of what had just happened. She sat back down at her desk, opened the envelope, and read.

Jennifer,

> *Last night I waited for sleep that seemed like it would never come. As I lay in bed, I had random thoughts of this or that, nothing of any major importance. Eventually, my thoughts drifted to you. That happens a lot lately.*
>
> *I have always considered my life a journey. Traveling from here to there, trying new things, just letting life happen. For an unexplained reason—some might say destiny, some may say luck—my travels brought me to you. We had seen each other several times over the years, but it was usually just polite conversation between two people preoccupied with life. However, this time was different. I felt compelled to reestablish our friendship. One night, when I felt like having a decent dinner and an intelligent conversation, I found myself asking you. You graciously accepted and off we went.*

That night I was enchanted by your smile. It gave the impression of innocence with a hint of mischief. Then I noticed your eyes, not the color, but beyond. They seemed sad as if they had weathered many storms. Yet they still retained an essence of determination. I found myself lost in them during dinner. You were talking but the world was silent for a moment. A long moment. I felt strange. Things deep inside of me, feelings buried deep down were suddenly touched.

After dinner I called a few times, but never had the courage to leave a message. When we did speak, I couldn't even get the words out, nothing seemed to make sense. Jennifer, I have never met anyone like you. I look at you and see someone who has not had it easy but who has endured and continues to push on with eagerness and determination. I want to know your dreams and hand them to you. I want to take your tears of sorrow and make them tears of joy. I want to show you the beautiful things I have seen and done. I want to make you smile as much as I can not only because I want to see you happy but also because when you smile it makes me feel truly amazing.

I'm not sure exactly why I wrote you this letter. I believe it's more or less because I feel the need to confess. I have no hidden agendas or ulterior motives, just a desire to let you know how good you make me feel. I want to make you feel as good you make me feel. I want to let you know I care.

Jason

The letter fell from Jennifer's hand and landed on her desk. Wow. She began to think back over the many years they had known each other.

Jason had come to her high school in Yakima, Washington, in his sophomore year. His father's job as a nuclear engineer had caused their family to move around the country his entire life. He had spent his childhood as the perpetual new kid, figuring things out for himself, always making new friends. Only this time, one part of his life had changed forever: his mother was no longer there alongside him. After a long, painful illness, she had succumbed to lymphoma. Though Jason was outgoing by nature, there was now an emptiness in his life that could never be filled.

Jason made friends easily and, within months, he began volunteering with the local fire brigade. And dating a quiet girl named Jennifer. She knew all too well the emptiness he felt. Her mother had died of leukemia when she was just nine. Until she met Jason, she was the only person she knew without a mom. Jennifer understood the pain Jason was feeling, the prospect of not having your mother there to help you with homework, get ready for the prom, walk through graduation or, someday, your wedding. Though neither could quite express what they were feeling, their shared tragedies had forged an unusual and unspoken bond.

One night the couple met at Jason's house to watch movies. Fifteen-year-old Jason sat beside his girlfriend, paying only partial attention to the movie, trying to figure out when would be the best time to give her a kiss. Realizing there was no perfect time, he just leaned over and did it. At first, Jennifer kissed him back, but the whole thing made her so nervous that she started to giggle. Jason was crushed. "I guess I'll take you home now," he sulked, positive she'd been laughing at his ability to smooch. By Monday a rumor was going around school. Jason wanted to break up. Though both wanted a second kiss, it would have to wait seven years.

After high school, Jennifer began dating the wonderful, loving man she would eventually marry. A wonderful and loving man, that is, until he began to drink.

Then he was out of control. Liquor released in him a monster that was always hovering just beneath his skin. In the beginning, Jennifer thought his alcoholism was something she could help him overcome—until one evening his anger raged out of control and he hit her across the face. Jennifer swallowed hard, the place where his hand had struck hot and stinging. Embarrassed by the predicament she found herself in, she told no one.

As far as Jennifer's family was concerned, there was no such thing as divorce. A marriage, no matter how bad, was meant to last forever. The third time her husband hit her, Jennifer called her dad in tears and asked if she could stay with him for the night. "Work it out," her father replied. Jennifer pleaded with him, finally admitting the secret she'd been keeping. "Work it out," he repeated before hanging up the phone.

The next morning, her husband brought her flowers, brought her gifts, apologized profusely, and swore he would never touch another drop. A few months later, the bottles returned. With or without her father's support, Jennifer wasn't waiting around for her husband's next outburst. Secretly, she began saving money. She kept her intentions to herself until she'd signed the lease on a new apartment. Within a day, she had moved out.

It took a long time for Jennifer to hold her head high. Every time she went out to meet with friends or go to church, Jennifer was positive people were snickering behind her back, waiting for her to make another mistake. She never discussed her broken marriage with anyone and didn't date for a year after her divorce was final. And when she did finally date, she did so with guarded emotions.

Jason Ray had had problems, too. A wildlands forest firefighter, Jason was back to the traveling life of his youth. His brigade was called to all parts of the country to battle blazes, often for weeks at a time. On one such occasion, he had returned to Yakima to find that his fiancée had left town, taking the ring he'd given her along with the contents of his bank account, and married another man. With hard work, Jason had adopted hard play. He was staying out late, experimenting with drugs, and, to keep him company in the party lifestyle, had taken up with a party girl who managed to rob him of more than his money. His self-esteem plummeted while his drug use escalated. He was in the process of getting his life back together when he met up with Jennifer again.

Jennifer. When he thought of the stunning beauty with long dark hair and forgiving eyes, he wanted to touch the part of her that was hurting—just as she had understood him when his mother died. He wanted to heal her pain as well as his own. The same girl who'd giggled at his kiss seven years before was the woman he now needed to know better. When he brought the letter and the flowers to her office that November day, he'd hoped for some kind of response. But Jennifer, protective of herself, said nothing. They spent Thanksgiving together, but still she made no mention of it, acting like the whole episode had never occurred. Jason told her that he cared for her, that he loved her, only to be met with a change of subject. Jennifer didn't retract her friendship, though, and the two would often catch a movie or dinner together. Finally, tired of being rejected, he called her. "I can't take this anymore," he told her, his voice cracked with emotion. "I need to know how you feel." She tried to explain that she cared for him, that she needed time, but the words came out in a sputtering mess. "I have to go," Jason said and hung up the phone.

Having assumed that Jason wanted to end whatever shred of a relationship they had, she sat down to write. Boyfriends had always told her she was a hard person to love, that she pushed people away, and Jennifer had started to believe it. Now, she realized she only needed the right person to love. And he had given up on her. An hour later she called him back to tell him she had something for him. He immediately drove to her apartment and when Jennifer opened the door, she handed him the letter. Wordlessly, Jason took it from her hands and returned to his car.

Jason,

> *I'm restless. I reread the letter you gave
> me. If only you could remember what it said.
> The promises you made me. How did this all
> go so wrong? I was hurting and I still am. I
> needed to be loved and held, I wanted to hold
> you and let you feel that everything was going
> to be fine as long as we had each other. Yet I
> don't know how.*

> *On the phone tonight, I tried to tell you
> how I feel. Unloved, unwanted, just as I do
> now. I let my vulnerable side completely take
> over then I quickly stopped and apologized,
> but it was too late.*

> *I'm a hard person to love, I warned you
> of that more than once. I have always felt you
> would be the one to break down this wall I
> have built. Now, just as the last bit of the
> wall was coming down and your beautiful
> warm light started to fill that empty cavern
> and I believed that I could love you forever,*

*that I was going to be better and try
harder . . . it all fell apart. You walked away
with every last bit of hope I had. Now, there is
nothing.*

*People make mistakes, they learn from
them and go on. They become better. I made a
mistake, many in fact. I said I was sorry and
you walked away. People have treated you
badly many times. I am afraid to love you. I
came from a broken life and it has taken a
long time for me to give my heart to you, for
me to even try. But just as we're fighting the
last stretch, you gave in, you don't want to go
on. You have to fight for the love that you
want and when you are tired and have
nothing left, get up and keep fighting because
in the end, I* promise *you it will be worth
every step on the way.*

*Remember this: when you find the girl of
your dreams, don't let her go. Fight for each
other. The passion will be stronger than any
you have ever felt because you gave every
ounce of yourself. Don't make each other pay
for the mistakes of people who wronged you in*

the past. Start fresh and never look back. This is the lesson I have learned tonight.

Jen

Jason folded the letter, leaned his head against the steering wheel, and cried. He didn't want to give up. All he needed to know was that she cared and now he knew. He got out of the car and knocked on Jennifer's door.

Now that he had a reason to stay put, Jason quit the wildlands brigade. The closest job he could find was in a town ninety miles away. He lived at the station for seven months, returning for weekend visits. They wrote each other nearly every day they were apart.

In the letter below, Jennifer congratulates Jason on turning his life around and thanks him for simply being himself.

Jason,

As I lay here thinking about you, I recall the way your eyes portray your feelings so easily. That's why I love you so much, you give yourself freely to me. A gift no one has ever entrusted me with before.

113
◆

I love you, not only for what you've done with your life, but for what you're doing to mine. I see it everyday. You have made me happy and whole. Without a word, without a gesture, without a doubt, just by being yourself. Such a simple thing yet the hardest to give.

I guess that's why a love like ours is wonderful but also frightening. We give everything. So much so that it would seem one could not survive without the other.

I live only to return to your arms at the end of the day. How could I ever explain to another person what joy this brings me? How can I describe the overpowering sense of love when wrapped in those protective arms? I would give anything for you to know how it feels. To know that at times when I think about the love we share, I can't stop the tears from falling. How strange, that during all those times in my life when I cried it was tears of sadness. Only since you came into my heart do I cry tears of joy.

All my love,
Jennifer

Jason's reply was just as heartfelt. It was a promise to love her forever.

Jennifer,

> *I was sitting here unable to sleep so I thought I would write you a letter. I cannot begin to tell you how wonderful you have made my life the last several months. Months . . . I am at a loss for time. It is as if everything from the stars in the heavens to the flowers in the fields has stopped in time to witness us discovering each other. Every moment with you is like a breath of crisp fresh air. It kindles every sense in my body and soul. It stirs me like an autumn wind rustles the leaves. It is an awakening to the realization that I have found a love that knows no boundaries.*

> *I may never be very successful or be able to spoil you with gifts, but I can and I will give you every ounce of the love I feel for you, every last breath of my soul. All that I am is yours. I am not here to tease you, I am not here to obtain you, I'm not here to patronize*

you or tell you I can relate when I cannot. I am not here to lie to you or fill you with half-truths about myself. I am only here to love you, protect you, and try to make every tomorrow better than each yesterday. You have forever changed my perception of love and life and, to top it all off, despite my short-comings, you love me back.

116
◆

Forever yours,
Jason

"When are you going to marry me?" Jason teased her on one of his weekend visits in 1998. "In the year 2000," she replied with a sly glance. As they began to plan their wedding, Jennifer could not help but think of her first trip to the altar. Having been surrounded by family and friends only illuminated the fact that one person was missing: her mother. Jason also felt a large wedding would be painful without his mom. They decided to wed not at their church or even in their town, but on the beach in Jamaica, just the two of them. Before leaving, Jennifer got a call from her dad. He wished her a good flight, reminded her to call once she got there to let him know she was safe. His advice to

"work it out" with her first husband had left their relationship strained. Before hanging up the phone, he
asked her, "If you could change anything in your life,
would you?" To her amazement, Jennifer answered no.
The lessons she had learned were painful, but she
wouldn't change a thing. She had stayed true to herself
regardless of what others told her was the "right thing to
do." She had stopped worrying about what others
thought. She believed in herself, had learned to love herself. From the ashes of that first marriage, a stronger
Jennifer had emerged. And now she could share her
once-wizened self with a man deserving of her affections. Though he never apologized, her father knew he
had been wrong. "I'm proud of you," he told his daughter. "You made the right decision."

On the white sand beaches of Jamaica, Jennifer and
Jason were married. Just the two of them. Each had
written a letter to the other for the ceremony, promises
to last an eternity.

Letters that say lovely things when there is no occasion requiring such expressions can bring the purest kind of delight. If you never know when such a letter—perhaps just a note left where you will find it unexpectedly—is going to turn up, the small joyous jolt of surprise it provides can make your day. That is all the more true when your love has survived great difficulties.

Making it Last

Rebecca Barrett and Thomas Stokes met in the spring of 1970 at the Arctic Circle drive-in theater in Salmon, Idaho. She was sixteen, in her junior year of high school. Spotting a few friends in a parked car, Becky went over to say hello. In the backseat sat a man she'd never seen before. Never one to be shy, Becky leaned into the car. "Who's the good-looking guy?" she asked with the moxie only a sixteen-year-old can muster. Luckily, the attraction was mutual. Tom liked this young lady's assertive tone. Here this sixteen-year-old girl had confidence when, at the same exact time, Tom's confidence in his decisions, in himself, was faltering. He was twenty-two, and had just been discharged from the air force. While he was serving in the military, his marriage had fallen apart, and he was in the process of getting a divorce. Was it that he had married too young? Sometimes he thought so.

Becky and Tom spent that first evening ignoring the movie and getting to know each other. As Becky returned home with her older brother Dan late that night, she told her brother, "I'm going to marry that man." Dan assured her she was jumping the gun, thinking about marriage at her age. "No," Becky asserted, "I'm going to marry him."

The last thing Tom was looking for was a relationship. Especially with a girl six years his junior. But there was something irresistible about Becky Barrett. The next time he saw her, she was in the passenger seat of her best friend, Toni Scoble's, 1958 Chevrolet. Like the rest of the kids their age, the girls were "dragging" Main Street—driving up and down the road, stopping for sodas, listening to music, and seeing who was there. As they passed, Tom caught a glimpse of the saucy girl he'd met at the drive-in and flagged them over to the side of the road. He chatted with the girls for a minute then told them the big news: his divorce was nearly final. Becky and Tom started going steady that night.

One Saturday in May of 1970, Tom drove his Matador Red 1969 Plymouth GTX into town to pick up Becky. Along with several friends, they spent a day at nearby Williams Lake boating and fishing. Back at school on the Monday following the trip to the lake, Becky opened her notebook and was surprised to find a note—the *first* note—from Tom.

To the Most Wonderful Person I Know,

Hi, it's only me. But then, you know me don't you? I'm that rare specimen you discovered the other morning at the lake.

*There are lots of us men around but not many
in the species of* Tomlax-hugsnkissez. *The*
Tomlax-hugsnkissez *is nurtured by a yearly
rainfall of caring, truth, and appreciation and
he is usually found in an area of great warmth
and lots of loving caresses. Given these things
generously for over a period of eternity, the*
Tomlax-hugsnkissez *will return love and
service to you with a money-back guarantee if
not completely satisfied (kisses, however, are
nonrefundable). Please sign on the dotted line
if in agreement:*_____

123
◆

As the months went on, the couple found themselves spending all of their free time together. Every time
Becky was near him, her heart raced. Every time Tom
was near her, he couldn't help but smile. They started
talking about getting married, and Tom made it official
with a letter of proposal. He began the letter with a
quote from a famous poem by Elizabeth Barrett Brown-
ing, "How do I love thee? Let me count the ways," and
went on to tell Becky the ways in which he loved her.

*You may count these ways as though you were
to count the waves of every ocean on this*

planet when they grace the shores of continents, as they span the globe. Their beauty only second to yours.

May the forces of love in their innumerable consistencies forever be in your presence. I, being one of those forces, ask your hand and soul in a life of unity.

It is possible for two people to possess a love and oneness beyond their wildest dreams. I know this and I pray that from this day forth, I will be your thoughtful companion. That I will be the one to bring you happiness, the one to bring you contentment in all facets of life no matter how wonderful or how dire the situation. Let us go one extra step in our devotion.

Though he had proposed to her, Tom didn't present Becky with an engagement ring until Christmas of that year. When she opened the box, she couldn't believe her eyes. It was a gold flower with a diamond set in the middle. *This is impossible*, she thought then turned to Tom in bewilderment. "How on earth?" Tom had no idea what Becky was talking about, had no idea that Becky had seen the same ring at the local jeweler only weeks

124
•

before and had fallen in love with it. "That's the ring I want," she had whispered to herself, staring at the ring through the jeweler's window, her words fogging up the glass. Perplexed by her question and dying to know what she thought of her gift, Tom said, "Well, do you like it?" Becky let out a scream, pounced on Tom, and smothered his face with kisses.

The young couple went straight to the Barrett residence to ask Becky's father's permission. Standing in the living room, Tom took a deep breath and looked Wayne Barrett in the eye. "May I have your daughter's hand?"

Wayne Barrett looked at his daughter as if to ask if this was for real. Becky proudly displayed the third finger on her left hand where the gold flower engagement ring sat.

"Take that off," her father said.

Becky and Tom were forbidden to see each other. Looking back, Becky can laugh at the teen-movie aspects of the next several months: the furtive meetings arranged with the help of friends, the endless little lies that had to be told, the added excitement of being together when it was forbidden. She particularly remembers their closest call, which occurred one evening at the place where it all began, the Arctic Circle drive-in. "Tom and I were in the car making out. We don't know how long they had been there, but at some point, my parents had pulled up right alongside us. Lucky for us, they didn't recognize Tom's car. They were too busy making out themselves!" She laughs at the irony. "I slid down the seat and crouched on the floor of the car, my heart ready to leap out of my chest, as Tom slowly pulled out of the parking space with the headlights off." The young couple got away undetected. Did Becky ever tell her parents about that night at the drive-in? "Oh, sure," she says easily, "but not until *years* later."

Becky and Tom continued to secretly see each other without raising suspicion. But in the summer of 1971, they had no choice but to admit what had been going on. Becky walked into the living room and stood beside the couch where her father sat watching Johnny Carson on TV. "Dad," she began, "I want to marry Tom." Wayne looked up from the TV. Didn't he get rid of that guy? The look of confusion on her father's face scared her. He'd been unjust toward Tom, but he was her father and he deserved to know the truth. "Dad, I'm pregnant." Without a word, Mr. Barrett turned back to the TV screen and continued to watch *The Tonight Show* while Becky stood frozen, waiting for his response. Minutes passed this way, and Becky was prepared for the worst. When credits started rolling on the television screen, he was ready to talk. "Becky," he began in an even tone, "you know how much I love you. If you want to marry

Tom, I'll support you. If you don't want to marry him and have the baby anyway, I'll support you. If you want to put it up for adoption, I'll support you. Whatever you want to do, I'll support you."

"I lost my father a few years ago," Becky says now, very quietly, "but I'll never forget that moment. It's one of the greatest memories I have of him."

127

Becky and Tom were married on June 25, 1971, one month shy of her eighteenth birthday, at the Fourth Square Church in Salmon. Becky and Tom bought a house in nearby Heyburn, Idaho. Their daughter Teresa came six months later, on December 15. They were so broke that first year that they couldn't afford to exchange Christmas gifts. "The only thing we got came from my mother," Becky says of that holiday season. "An orange plastic portable radio. We had a teeny, tiny Christmas tree in a coffee can," she laughs. "Our baby Teresa was our Christmas present." Aside from the small tree and the new bundle of joy, there was one more gift for the new Mrs. Stokes: a letter from her husband describing the Christmas he wished he could have given her.

Dearest Becky,

You may as well brace yourself for a very romantic letter because I'm feeling very much in love tonight. More than yesterday, less than tomorrow. I have been thinking about you all day at work. I missed you a lot.

128
◆

I can see your sweet, beautiful face in a dim light. There is soft music and the aroma of delicious food on a table flooded in candlelight, places set for two. Long-stemmed crystal glasses await the host and hostess to caress their salted brims and sip the smooth tartness of blended ice, tequila, and lime. The room is very dim, with dark carpet adding the touches of softness. Flames leap wildly from a fireplace with a bench hearth surrounding the front. Large glass sliding doors frame the lavish stillness of a first snowfall on the frozen lake.

I sit beside you, your head on my shoulder. Your long golden-brown hair glistens as the light from the flames caress your immaculate face, your large, beautiful gray and brown eyes sparkling in its refracted light. I caress your forehead and stroke your beautiful hair, its luster enhanced each time my hand passes. The crystal chimes softly as

*we share a toast to our happy future together
as man and wife and family. We sip slowly,
the spirits enhancing our already love-
warmed souls. I take you closer in my arms.
Dreams and fantasies come to mind as the
future stretches forward. Dreams
accompanied only by an occasional soft
whisper in each other's ears, "I love you . . . I
love you . . ."*

129
◆

*"I'm in the Mood for Love," plays on the
stereo. We both smile in silent agreement,
sealing our thoughts of unison with a kiss
from our hungry lips, moist and salty and
warm. You smile, like sunshine in this
darkened room. Your lips tell of love, of
experiences, of beauty within. A precious
moment of charm, a graciousness that comes
only to those of a true God, of a true Heaven,
envisioned in hearts of lovers.*

*I only ask to preserve this moment forever
and to make this woman happy beyond her
wildest dreams. To give her the proper love
and care and the delight of our relationship as
husband and wife: children. I wish to give her*

*security, a fine home to entertain friends and
to grow as a family. I will provide for her
safety and protection, strong arms to encircle
her when she is disappointed, a strong shoulder onto which she may fall asleep at night.
Our closeness evident, ever absorbing each
other in the stillness of our private chamber of
happiness and resolve: our bedroom. Softly I
whisper, "Good night my love," and say ever
more softly, "I love you, I love you, I love you."*

*Merry First
Christmas with
Love, Tom*

When she thinks about Christmas of 1971, Becky remembers it as the best. "Difficult, but the best."

Things went along smoothly at the house in little green and white Heyburn. In October of 1974, Becky gave birth to their second child, Matthew. Two children, three bedrooms, both Tom and Becky employed (he in construction, she managing a photography studio), but after six years of marriage what started out as a small hole soon began to unravel their relationship. Becky began to feel resentful, began to feel she had been pushed into a marriage. "Not only that," she says, "but I was so young that I never made a clean break from my family. I was still their little girl and then I was Tom's wife, the kids' mother. I didn't even know myself. How could I know Tom?"

Unable to reconcile their differences, Tom and Becky separated. Tom moved out and took a small apartment. They both flaunted their independence. "Calling each other names, staying out all night . . . we tried anything we thought would hurt the other person. Finally, we gave up and filed for divorce," Becky remembers. They were tired of fighting, fed up with caring, and ready to call it quits. Even though neither of them was convinced divorce was the right thing, they weren't getting along and didn't know what else to do. Maybe it wasn't the perfect answer, but at least it was an answer.

As a last effort to salvage their marriage, they decided to spend a week alone. "We were going to get a divorce," Becky says. "What did we have to lose?" They'd heard Bend, Oregon, was a quiet place to visit. They left the kids with friends in Idaho and set off.

Once they checked into the hotel, the pace of life slowed to a much-needed crawl. Without children or parents, friends, gossip, phones, or siblings, the couple could finally let go. When asked what they did, the answer is simple, "Talked and walked." It was there in

Bend, amid the juniper bushes and ponderosa pines, that the couple finally got to know each other again. They talked openly about Tom's jealousy, how he'd been hurt in the past. They spoke of Becky's resentment of their early marriage. They had an unexpected conversation about sexual fantasies; each illuminating their secret desires with a newfound level of comfort. They had fun, they told stories, and they laughed. Without demands or ultimatums, they let it be known what each expected from their marriage, what wasn't working and what was. They talked about their lives together and what their lives would be like apart. They spoke in a way neither had ever taken the time to do before.

"Those were ten of the most wonderful days of our lives," she says. "It was then that I realized that I really loved Tom, that God wanted us to be together." With two days left before their separation became legally permant, they raced back to Idaho and halted the divorce proceedings. Within a few weeks they packed up everything in Heyburn, put the house on the market, and moved to Bend, where they still live today. "Strange to think we could have ended way back then," she says. "I recommend it to every couple: just leave everyone, get away, establish yourselves. Find your comfort zone."

Tom had always been the romantic one, and once they had found themselves again, he found a new way to express his love. He started writing her small love notes on three-by-five-inch pink cards, some two dozen of them over the next few years. He never gave them to her in recognition of a special occasion. Rather, they were left for her in honor of the day-to-day life they share. Becky has received "Pink Cards" in the mail, has found them in books, and under her pillow. This one was the first.

Becky,

This card expresses my every feeling for you that is too good for pen and ink to know. Those expressions of deepest love, devotion, children, thoughts, and happiness. The reason for the Passion Pink color doesn't need an explanation. With the love we share no explanation need accompany a card like this ever again. This card is us and everything we do! It is everything we will ever stand for that is intimate between you and me . . .

One spring morning, Becky went out into her garden and was shocked to find tulips blooming. She loved tulips but never remembered to plant them early enough. "Tom!" She ran back into the house, completely amazed and baffled at what was happening just outside her home. "There are tulips blooming in the garden!" With one smile he let her know it was he who had planted bulbs in the fall. But that's just one of the many romantic things he has done for her over the years. The letters below also show how far Tom will go to let Becky know that she is still "the one." In this letter from August of 1992, Tom reminisces about the first trip they ever took together—the trip to Williams Lake back in 1970.

I've heard talk of a mountain lake in central Idaho where two lovers sit in the cool early morning air and the water, still as a mirror, echoes the call of a loon.

The sounds they make, the words they speak, are nearly twenty-one years old. But I can hear it now, fresh and clear as if today were then . . . a time of red Plymouths, Pink Cards, and peanut M&Ms.

But today is not so different. Plymouths still come in red, the cards are still pink, and M&Ms never go out of style. I want to list for you in a chain that won't be written in one day, a few reasons why I love you.

These links in the chain will appear

when least expected. Just know each one is
just for you.

And so, over the next few days, true to his promise, Tom left Becky a "chain" of little notes around their home.

Note 1: I like the way your lips tell me you
       love me, without words . . .

Note 2: I like the rhythm of your breathing
       when I touch your skin . . .

Note 3: I like the fragrance of Opium linger-
       ing on your bra when I remove it very
       slowly . . .

Note 4: I like the way you look at me side-
       ways, your chin tucked low, and
       touch me with your eyes . . .

That same year, Becky helped her sister move from Albuquerque, New Mexico, to Boise, Idaho. Ever the romantic, Tom placed a note in his wife's suitcase before she left. Though she was happy to find the note, Becky was not too surprised. She'd left one for him back in Oregon. "It's sort of a tradition," she says. "Whoever is going out of town finds a note in their suitcase and whoever is staying home finds one, too, usually under the bed."

Tom wrote this card to Becky on June 25, 1995, their twenty-fourth wedding anniversary.

136
◆

I've been giving a lot of thought to what I would like to tell you on our twenty-fourth Anniversary . . . but you already know how very much I love you and I decided to just say THANK YOU!

Thank you for the happiest twenty-four years of my life.

Thank you for always being there for me with love and encouragement.

Thank you for our wonderful children and the happy home that we were able to raise them in.

Thank you for the best and most creative lovemaking a man could ever desire!!!!!

Thank you for being my very best friend even though it was pretty hard sometimes.

Thank you for always being so supportive of me.

Thank you for never letting a day go by
where I didn't know how deeply you love me.
Thank you for the last twenty-four and
the next twenty-four. I'm looking forward to it.
I love you with all my heart.

It's now been thirty years since feisty Becky Barrett asked about the cute guy at the Arctic Circle drive-in and twenty-nine since she married him. Though the road has had its bumps and curves, neither Tom nor Becky would change a thing. "To say Tom and I love each other is an understatement," says the grandmother of four. "We have arrived at the point of 'living' each other."

Some letters remain forever unsent. There is the letter written in anger that the writer realizes, before it is too late, must not be mailed. There is the declaration of love that should not be made, at least not yet. And there are letters that would not have been written at all if they could be sent.

All That's Left

She was crossing the big noisy room, making her way through the boisterous dance-club crowd, one hand firmly clasping her roommate's. They didn't want to get separated in this mess. Roommates had to stick together when it was one of those nights that seemed to have brought out every unattractive guy in town—and all of them wanting to talk to *you*. Suddenly, out of nowhere, another hand slipped into her free one. And astonishingly, it felt as though it belonged there. Adrienne looked up to see who the hand belonged to. The man was very handsome, with dark hair and deep brown eyes that held hers with their warmth.

He danced with her. He danced with her roommate, not trying to leave her out. But it was Adrienne whose hand he had first grasped, and she soon began to hope that she could feel that special grip for a very long time to come.

M. is what she calls him now. Just the initial remains. Yet it had seemed it would be otherwise. They met in Seattle, where Adrienne was part of the music scene. Despite her French first name, she was very much an American. M. was an Arab, raised in Syria and Saudi Arabia. Adrienne knew the stereotypes that usually got applied to Arab men about their attitude toward women. But M. wasn't like that. "If we had different opinions on an issue, he always respected what I had to say, and I treated him with the same respect," Adrienne says. "He liked that about me."

M. talked to Adrienne about his family, about life in Saudi Arabia. Arranged marriages were quite common. Multiple marriages were permitted, but had not been the practice in M.'s family. "He has one mother, and both grandfathers had only one wife," Adrienne says. "But even if his family had practiced multiple marriage, it wouldn't have bothered me, because he told me he would never do that."

Although she had become deeply involved with M., Adrienne had to go to New Zealand to record a few dance tunes. "There was this understanding between us that when I returned we would get back together." And they did. So Adrienne was not unduly worried when M. left in November of 1999 for a long-awaited visit to his family, which he hadn't seen in four years, in Saudi Arabia. He and Adrienne had been together two years by then. She had gone abroad, and come back, and they had taken up where they left off. He was going home for a visit, that was all, and then they would be together again.

A week later, M. telephoned her from Saudi Arabia. The sound of his voice was so nice to hear that it took her a moment to understand what he was saying, what was happening. He had quit his job in Seattle without telling her. "I've decided to stay here," he said. As she listened in stunned silence, M. told her that his mother had found a woman for him to marry. Adrienne's heart raced. "You're . . . you're not going to do it, are you?" she asked in a shaky voice. For a moment he said nothing. Then he said that he had to get off the phone.

143
◆

Adrienne would subsequently go over the conversation she had had with M. about arranged marriages and multiple wives. She had been sure he meant that he would not be a party to either of those arrangements, but now she realized that he had been talking only about multiple wives. "I suppose he felt he was doing the right thing," she says. "*For them.*"

When M. had left for his visit home, he had not given Adrienne an address where he could be reached. And she had not asked.

Now it was too late. He was gone.

As Adrienne tried to work through her pain and confusion, she wrote a letter that would never be sent.

Dearest M.,

If I could get this to you now, it would be to tell you I miss you. I would tell you I have

*moved on . . . but only because of the human
need for human contact. Only for this. I
would tell you that when you left the country
it hurt me deeply. What hurt more, though, is
that you left without a trace, so that I couldn't
find you.*

144
•

*Ours was a young, timeless love. It was
passionate and intense and tender. You were
my best friend. You treated me better than
anyone ever has, before or since. I laughed
more with you than I ever have. I would have
you know—if I had a place to send this—that
every day I have tried to feel. I haven't had
any true emotions, beyond those inspired by
daily life, since you left six months ago.*

*I write by the light of a candle given to
me by a beau who wants me to move away
with him and make a new start. This is the
second such offer I've had in the past month.
It's flattering and romantic, and I am
considering taking him up on it. The only
thing that stops me is that I would have to
give up the last flicker of hope of you. I know
that I must, however, and that you would
want me to go on and achieve my dreams.*

"Don't give yourself to just anyone," you said. "Don't let them touch you." I won't, I promised. No one has touched my heart and soul since. No one could. I cried every night for so long, and my deepest emotions escaped with those tears. The only emotion I can still feel is confusion. I have tried and will continue to try to find my way out of the spinning dizziness and into stability.

You chose to return to a place where arranged marriages are still common and to embrace this tradition. I can't tell you this was wrong because only you can know what is right for you. But I can't escape the feeling that it would not have worked if you had made me your wife. "I will be watched," you said. "It's strict there." I can't help wondering if you are happy in a new life in which your freedom is limited, with a new wife who does what you say. I've never just followed orders; that is what you loved about me, that I didn't do what you said. This I know. You came a long way to find me and I'll never forget it. I would like to thank you for allowing me the pleasure of knowing you as much and for as

*long as you could let me. The beauty and the
truth of my feelings for you are enough to
sustain me for a lifetime. Thank you for how
you changed me.*

*Before meeting you, I was a girl who loved
her freedom. Now I am again . . . but now I
know how it feels to deeply love and to be loved
deeply. You are the one who wouldn't steal my
freedom and the only one I would have allowed
to do so. I can't resent you for leaving because I
understand. I love you even more.*

*As I finish this letter, I seal my heart
against ever loving so deeply again, for I know
it's not possible in a lifetime. As I put out this
candle, I extinguish the hope of ever seeing you
again, and let the heaviness of my heart dissi-
pate with the smoke. I release you into the happiness I can only imagine. I will walk alongside
you in my heart for the rest of my life.*

Love Forever,
Adrienne

M.'s hand had slipped into hers out of nowhere. He
had slipped away just as quietly.

A letter of apology is one thing—
often it can be quite brief and to the
point. But a letter of true contrition requires the
writer to dig a lot deeper, to own up to the failures
and hurts that lie beneath the surface. A letter of
contrition means being honest with oneself
beyond the incident of the moment.

Betting on Love

After a few weeks of dating, Bryan had the courage to tell her about his diabetes. "That's why I'm so thin," he explained to her. "My growth was stunted as a kid and I feel full when I haven't eaten for a whole day. But I should eat. I mean, it's really dangerous for me not to eat. But I don't ever feel like it. The doctors," he admitted, "are always on my case about it." The woman looked at Bryan and coolly replied, "I already have two kids," as if he hadn't noticed. "I don't need a third."

Fed up with dating, Bryan confided in his best friend, Bob. "That's it, man," Bryan grumbled. "No more women. I'm just a bachelor." Bob had a hard time believing such a stupid statement. "Okay then, let's make a bet," Bryan said gamely. "Whichever one of us gets married first has to buy the other one a trip to Hawaii." The men shook on it. Bryan thought he was a cinch to get to Hawaii. Every girl Bob dated was certifiably nuts, but one of them would no doubt get him down the aisle. Bryan, on the other hand, was convinced he was destined to be a loner.

How could any woman want him? A person with medical problems, a man who wouldn't eat. The diabetes was an obstacle, a condition that wears down the body with time, but it wasn't debilitating. It didn't stop him from working, from taking classes at the local junior college, or enjoying the outdoors. But when he thought about that horrible date with that horrible woman, the smug and dismissive way she treated him, his heart sank and his anger flared. Unlovable. Alone. Everytime his thoughts turned toward sour, he could feel his skin hardening to thick armor. He wanted to fight back, but there was no one to fight—he refused to let anyone in. No matter, he was committed to bachelorhood. Quick to prove his point to himself, to Bob, and anyone else who thought differently, he put up a profile on Love@AOL. *Nobody will respond*, he thought, *and that will be the end of that*. Besides, he certainly wasn't buying Bob a plane ticket to Hawaii. Below his protective layer, Bryan wanted to be wrong.

He had all but forgotten about the profile until a week later when he received a few responses. One woman seemed all right, but she lived too far away from Bryan's Sacramento home. Another didn't like the outdoors and the third one smoked. Hadn't they read what he had written? He wanted someone close by. He loved boating, camping, and fishing. Having felt like his partying days were behind him, Bryan had given up drugs, alcohol, and tobacco. He preferred quiet evenings to parties, reading science fiction to going to bars. In his profile, he'd written that he didn't mind dating a woman who already had kids and that he someday wanted a family of his own. And here all these women seemed just the opposite. At this rate, it was obviously Bryan who'd be traipsing the beaches and shouting "Aloha!" Then he got an e-mail from Kimberly.

She and Bryan shared the same interests, liked the same music. She didn't drink or smoke. She had a one-year-old daughter and adored animals. They e-mailed each other a few times and even Bryan had to admit there was chemistry. Every word she wrote he found himself nodding in agreement with. Every joke she typed made him laugh. After a few days, the e-mail turned to phone calls—*long* phone calls—and the phone calls led to plans to meet in person. On his way out the door to meet her at the train station, Bryan stopped at the mirror to comb his hair. He'd sent Kim a picture and she said she liked his long hair. Kim then sent a picture of herself to Bryan and he adored her round cheeks. Every time they'd spoken on the phone he felt more and more comfortable, wanted. He pulled his hair into a ponytail. "This," he said to his reflection, "will never work."

Kim got off the train, scanning the crowd for the face from the picture. *This is crazy*, she thought. *We've only been in contact for two weeks!* But then again, it was in her nature to be impetuous. Whenever she decided

151
•

she didn't like a job, she had no qualms about quitting. When she had found out she was pregnant, she kept the baby even though she wasn't in a committed relationship. And everything had always worked out for the best, hadn't it? So when Bryan suggested she visit, she jumped on the next train. She was nervous but didn't care. She liked this guy and therefore it *had* to be right.

152

Bryan approached her and timidly pecked her on her soft cheek. He'd been so tense about meeting her that he'd forgotten to plan anything for them to do. They walked back to his apartment and never stopped talking. *This is unreal,* Bryan thought, feeling his protective armor melt away. By the time Sunday rolled around, he had already taken Kim to meet his parents and was discussing the big "forever." "We'd gotten along so well," he says now, "that it wasn't a matter of 'should we get married' but '*when* should we get married.'" They took an evening stroll down by the Sacramento River. Without apprehensions, Bryan proposed to Kim. When the last train left the station that night, it departed without Kim.

With such a whirlwind romance, there was bound to be an uproar. First, there were Bryan's parents, who thought the pair were being silly and irresponsible. Then there were Kim's parents, who wanted to know just how Bryan planned on being a stepfather to their granddaughter, a child he'd never met. But Kim was firm. Having already quit her job, she went back home to Stockton, packed her things, and got her daughter. She knew what she wanted and that was Bryan. Nothing could stop her.

It seemed everyone was telling them what to do, even Bob. He didn't even care about his trip to Hawaii! All along he knew neither he nor Bryan could afford such a ludicrous bet. And in the midst of it all sat Bryan and Kim. It felt as though they were in the middle of a storm, the words "no" and "impossible" and "ridiculous" beating on them like heavy rain. Tired of listening to others' opinions about what they considered the only option, they jumped in the car and headed to Lake Tahoe. They found a lakeside chapel that would marry them that afternoon. Just before the ceremony began, Kim called her best friend back home. "Hold this," Kim said to one of the witnesses, handing over her cell phone. With the phone turned toward the minister, her best friend back in Stockton could hear every word. Kim was ready to become Mrs. Dimig.

Kim's dad had always dreamed of walking his daughter down the aisle. Bryan's mother had wanted to help plan her son's wedding. But Bryan and Kim had eloped and all of that was now gone. What remained were two happy people, now husband and wife. But they would persevere and grow with each other's help. Kim

153
•

has learned all she can about diabetes. She goes with Bryan to all his doctor visits and makes sure he eats regular meals, even when he doesn't want to. Bryan is learning to become vulnerable to Kim. The letter below was written after an argument. There had been a misunderstanding about plans and Kim had been late, a small mistake that had snowballed into angry words.

154

7/25/95

My Darling Kimberly,

I feel terrible when we fight. You tell me that I pick fights, that I look for them. I'm going to try not to let little things get to me so much. I'm going to try not to blow things out of proportion. I'll need your help.

For the past ten or twelve years, I've tried not to feel anything. When I was forced to deal with emotion, it was usually anger. For me, anger is the most familiar, comfortable emotion, because it's the devil that I know. You've opened up a whole new world to me. You've opened up feelings to me that I didn't really believe myself capable of. I knew I was able to be hurt but I didn't really believe I could be so much in love. I thought the drugs and alcohol had burned that capability out of me.

I was so convinced I'd never marry. But along with this most powerful emotion called love, all my other feelings have begun to emerge from the deep place where I had hidden them so many years ago. I suddenly find myself to be a person of powerful emotions. It's a new experience for me, having something inside pulling me this way and that.

Now I think I'm almost hypersensitive. Love, anger, jealousy, insecurity, joy, sadness, pain, happiness are all there and at a level that I'm just not used to. As I write this letter, I feel a love for you that's so strong, it's almost painful. I sit here at my desk, missing you so much that I want to leave here and come home, right now! I want to touch you, be in your presence. As I've said before, the word "love" seems a pitiful label to describe my passion for you.

Now I look at anger as a familiar old friend, an emotion that I know how to deal with. My low opinion of myself causes a deep insecurity and fear that I'll lose you. And I'm

155
◆

pushed toward anger yet again. I need your support, my dearest, because I just can't be without you.

I need your help to prop up my sagging confidence. I need your patience while the childish part of me matures enough to stop trying to push you away, to stop testing the limits of your love. With you by my side, I'm ready to take on the universe and succeed in overcoming its difficulties. I really hope that the part of me that is picking these silly little fights, fights that nevertheless are painful, can be matured or banished before any serious damage is done. I know that with your help, these goals I have can be achieved, for our happiness. I love you, most beautiful of women, my beloved Kimberly, and I want only happiness for us.

Love and passion,
Bryan

Bryan admits that since he and Kim did not have a long courtship, they are getting to know each other now.

"What's great is that we are so committed," he says. "We both know that it's more difficult than if we were boyfriend and girlfriend. But the fact that we're married makes us work even harder at the relationship."

A year has passed since they eloped and Kim and Bryan have already renewed their vows. This time around they had a large wedding in Sacramento's Capital Park, where Kim's father proudly walked his daughter down the aisle. Two-year-old Amanda was the flower girl. From the park they rode to the river, the same river where Bryan had proposed, in a horse-drawn carriage. There, friends and family awaited them on a boat for the reception. Bob was there, too, but unfortunately for him, the boat didn't have Hawaii as its destination.

Sometimes a letter becomes a way to sum up how far you've come, a way of toting up life's balance sheet and putting a relationship in perspective. It may take note of goals that have yet to be fully realized, but it can be celebratory at the same time: "Look, we've come through!"

Where Your Heart Leads You

"What do you mean, 'unstable'?" Chris Hawkins asked the customs agent of the Canadian Border Patrol. Just because he'd moved out of his apartment, quit his job at a pizza parlor, spent all his money on a bus ticket from North Carolina to Calgary to stay with a woman he'd met on-line, the agent was calling him "unstable" and "unsuited for entry"? Didn't this guy know anything about sacrifice? About adventure? About love? Apparently not, and there was not a whole lot Chris could say to convince the agent otherwise. Chris Hawkins was denied entry to the country. *Great,* he thought, looking over the snowy plains, shoving his hands in his empty pockets, *now what?*

Carrie Osborne had always assumed on-line chatting was for strange and lonely people. But the people in the article that Carrie sat reading were neither strange nor lonely. They were like her: young, professional, busy with their lives. She entered a chat room for the first time later that week and was surprised at the various types of conversations people were having. They wrote to each other about books, music, problems they were having with their children or at work, they swapped jokes they'd heard and shared stories about themselves.

She chatted with carpenters, publishers, and stay-at-home moms. As the weeks progressed, she found herself talking more and more to one person in particular: Chris.

Neither was looking for romance on the Internet—they had never filled out a dating profile nor put up photos for potential mates—and in the beginning it was strictly friendship. He told her about his long-term goals, about the classes he was taking to learn about computers. As a member of a sales team for a large company, Carrie found her daily chats with Chris a relaxing escape from the pressures of work. After months of sending words into cyberspace, Chris asked if he could come for a visit. "I've never been to Canada before," he typed on the screen. "Of course," she wrote back, "of course, of course, of course!"

Once he stepped off the plane and she saw him in person, Carrie felt an undeniable stirring inside of her that told her she wanted to be more than friends. Did he feel the same? It only took a couple of days in each other's presence to understand they'd been falling for each other all along. As the week came to an end, they promised they'd see each other soon and, of course, there would be their on-line conversations. When Chris returned to Winston-Salem, nothing he was doing there compared to the tenderness he felt when he was with

162

Carrie. The Internet was no longer good enough. Determined to be by her side, three months after his visit he quit his job, put his belongings in storage, and began a cross-country journey that would take four days—only to be deemed "unstable" at the border.

The driver of the Greyhound bus saw Chris standing in the cold outside the doughnut shop near the checkpoint station. "Weren't you supposed to go into Canada?" he asked. Feeling foolish to ever think such an impetuous plan would work, Chris stared at the ground and told him about the denial. The driver offered to buy him a cup of coffee and Chris, having not even enough change for that, accepted. "I have to go to North Dakota," the driver said. "Know anybody there?" It was just the beginning of a string of examples of the kindness of strangers that Chris and Carrie would come to appreciate deeply. Chris didn't know anyone in North Dakota, but he did know someone in South Dakota. Well, not *know* in the conventional sense. There was a woman named Di who lived in a farmhouse there who he and Carrie knew from the on-line chat room. He gave her a call once he reached the bus station in North Dakota. She had an extra room.

He called Carrie from there. A gust of adrenaline swept through her, her mind whirled. *South Dakota, farmhouse, no money, he loves me, oh God, what should I*

163
◆

do? What on earth could she do except follow his example and let love rule? Never mind that the cost of the plane ticket would wipe out her bank account, she quit her job, he booked her a flight from Calgary, and Carrie was on her way.

Snow fell from the sky in abundance. So much so that the plane was rerouted from South Dakota to Nebraska. Carrie called Chris to tell him the bad news. "Don't worry," he assured her, though he had no idea what to do next. He'd already come this far, how could a little snow stop him now? After the storm calmed, he borrowed Di's car and headed for the airport as fast as he could. Once they were in each other's arms again, Chris and Carrie forgot about the odds that were stacked against them. They were without jobs, a place to live, or money. They weren't able to return to Canada and they certainly couldn't stay in South Dakota forever. Like two corks bouncing in the sea, they might bob from wave to wave—but they would never sink, of that they were sure.

There was one issue, however, that they could not ignore: Carrie's depression. She'd been diagnosed by a doctor in Canada and had been taking medication, albeit with side effects. With her depression, her moods would swing up and down. With the medication, she was up all the time. So up it bordered on manic. And that was not the way she wanted her life to be, especially now that she had Chris.

They spent that winter in a small unheated shack behind Di's farmhouse, love the only thing to keep them warm. Heat or no heat, both were positive they'd made the right choice. On Christmas day, Carrie called home and was met by hostility. "Get back here!" her father demanded with a mixture of anger at the situation and fear for his daughter's fragile emotional state. They argued vehemently until Carrie hung up and sobbed into Chris's arms. "Sometimes you do what you have to do," he told her. "And we have to do this."

Their heart-driven journey would lead them back to North Carolina to live with Chris's family. One year after their reunion that snowy day in Nebraska, the two set a date to marry. A week before the wedding, Carrie wrote Chris this letter chronicling their journey of the heart.

Dearest Chris,

Once upon a space in time, our souls first did touch. We were alone, apart—but together in love. Our words danced in beautiful love letters and photos and memories across the electronic tide, but it was

our hearts that spoke and listened, that smiled
a million smiles and shed a million tears.
Worlds apart, we prayed under the same stars.
I always knew that you understood and
accepted me, but mostly you loved me, simply,
and without remorse, regret, or conditions.

166

Your arms held me tight long before we
touched and I felt safe. Then it happened.
Your journey to me fell short in complications.
What you must have been thinking, stranded
in South Dakota, cold, alone, and penniless.
When you called to tell me, I could not believe
my ears. And there you were, reassuring me
that everything would be fine!

And you were right.

We made it through, we found a way. A
hard road to come from the choices we made
that Sunday night. I was in Canada, not
doing well, and life had gotten so complicated.
You said you would take care of everything.
And you did.

As I boarded that plane, my heart knew
what my mind could not translate and a calm
descended. I knew I would be forever safe in

your arms. Two flights and I was in Omaha.
You were snowed in and could not get to me. I
was so alone and inexplicably calm,
surrounded by your reassuring love. I knew
you would make it. I knew we would make it.
Why? You promised me. And that's all it took.

South Dakota now: we slept on the floor, 167
an unheated farmhouse room, the hardwood
digging into our sides. The cold was piercing,
hot tears ran down our cheeks. But how warm
were we, wrapped in love? I remember helping
you tape up the windows in that room—
trying in vain to keep the cold at bay. I
remember Christmas, just us two. So sad and
lonely until we began our own traditions. We
played board games and sang Christmas
songs together. We didn't even have enough
money to exchange cards. We opened gifts
from our parents until we cried and shared
our dreams for our future. Still, I knew we
would make it. You promised me.

Three days on a bus, oh boy. We had
almost ten dollars in change. Thank goodness
for that two for one hamburger sale! And the

lovely woman who selflessly bought me a bottle of water, gave me her last pack of cigarettes, when she herself did not have much. Down to $3 and we'd seen so many towns. The bus wasn't so bad after all, once we discovered that you can cuddle well in those seats. One more day until a new beginning . . .

I finally had a moment for a sponge bath in the Nashville bus station. It felt like a bubble bath in the most exclusive hotel! We made it to Winston-Salem, to much nicer weather and your family. How wonderful they were to us, to me. I can still see the look on your face as you embraced your brother that morning we got off the bus—so happy to finally be home. I have learned how important his love is to you, and how you not only love me without conditions—but everyone.

More hard days to come. Depressed, I was incapable of taking care of myself and I was so far away from everything I had known. You took over again. Two jobs, long hours, green cards, visas, that nice fellow from the congressman's office helping us, and the first time we had money again. You brought me daisies. The most beautiful flowers I had ever seen. You could not have touched my soul more with the most expensive roses. We started saving and we sacrificed and we spoke of our future and were making it.

169
•

Off to a garage sale or to the Goodwill store to see our good friend there who always had a special something at a special price "that day, just for us." When I saw the rocking chair I wanted to take it home that day but couldn't afford it. We saved and patiently waited and hoped that it would not be sold. Fifteen dollars and three weeks later, I had my rocking chair, just as you had promised.

We were turned down at every apartment we looked at, we weren't a "good risk," they said. Then one landlord said yes. Finally, we were home.

The many long, late-night conversations about my illness and then to see it on TV:

Saint-John's-wort. How amazing to discover such a miracle in such an unlikely place. But that is sort of our story, isn't it? Miracles wrapped in struggle and sacrifice found in the most unlikely places. And months later, I am healthy, I am happy. All you have had to put up with and helped me through, such dark days when my strength left me. You have been my rock and truly my knight in shining armor. The strength you gave me to help heal my relationship with my family and the joy we shared when I was finally able to talk with them as a healthy person, these are gifts from your very soul. I thank you.

And I am thankful for the many friends we have made. Those who have been there loving us through some of the most difficult times. Both in our "real" life and the friends we have yet to hug in person. They have all touched us deeply.

Now as we begin our life together I know we will never forget where we have been. And I know that forever, we will make it, just as you promised.

*I love you. More than yesterday, less than
tomorrow.*

> *Forever and always,*
> *Carrie*

When Carrie wrote her letter to Chris just before
their wedding, she had no idea it would become a tradition. But it has. In the next letter, written on the eve
of their first anniversary, she relives the biggest surprise so far.

My Darling Chris,

*Here we are, one year married! It
seems like yesterday that we first started
exchanging friendly e-mails. Simply
friends—did we ever think it would become
more? I cannot recall. It seems to me that I
have loved you forever.*

*Not so long ago, we sat together
watching a line turn a very faint shade of
pink. "Do you see a line?" you asked. "I
think I see a line," I answered. "Better go get
another test."*

*Four tests and a day later—we had
several pink lines, bright as day.*

"We're going to have a baby," I sighed.

*We were worried but happy. Someone
planned it this way, just like our love. We have
learned to trust that everything in our life
happens for a reason, in it's own time. And it
has shown us that what happens always is for
the best.*

*Robert Casey Osborne-Hawkins, 9
pounds 4 ounces. A big name for a big boy. A
very special name, for an incredibly special
boy. The most important person in our lives.*

*Happy Anniversary, love. Here's to many,
many more years and tears and smiles and
laughter.*

*Here's to putting the mail back in the box and
locking the door when we know it's only bills.
We know they're not going to get paid until
payday—so why stress ourselves?*

Here's to compromise and respect.

*Here's to taking me out for chocolate when it
was all I wanted for dinner.*

*Here's to returning to the store an hour later
because it* wasn't *all I wanted for dinner!*

*Here's to finding a new apartment good
enough for three.*

*Here's to making each other laugh and being
able to say, "I'm sorry" quickly after any
argument . . . and mean every word.*

173

*Here's to late-night Walmart trips—just
because I needed something to do and to
pushing me in the wheelchair down the store
aisles the last few weeks of pregnancy.*

*Here's to the beautiful blue topaz necklace you
presented to me after Casey was born.*

*Here's to feeling for the baby as we drift off
to sleep.*

*Here's to giving up the new parts you wanted
for the computer so that we could buy the rest
of the baby stuff right now!*

*Here's to the 7 A.M. feedings and letting
me sleep.*

*Here's to washing the bottles and nipples and
for making my coffee in the mornings.*

Here's to the little conversations I have caught you having with Casey. You thought I was sleeping, didn't you?

Here's to bringing me daisies.

174
•

We have emerged as a family, stronger than ever. Carrie, Chris, and Casey: our family, our life.

I love you—still more than yesterday and less than I will tomorrow.

> *Forever and*
> *always,*
> *Carrie*

Just as her letter states, Carrie, Chris, and Casey have emerged as a strong family. Now married for three years, they are currently living in Arlington, Virginia, where Chris works as a computer systems analyst for a large law firm. Carrie, a stay-at-home mom, has healed her relationship with her family. They have come to love Chris just as much as she. And nobody, not even the Canadian Border Patrol, could ever call that unstable!

Even after many failures at love, it is still possible to find a new beginning. That new beginning may even reach far back into the past. Rediscovery can bring an extraordinary sense of freshness and hope that makes a wedding letter celebrating a new future almost imperative.

Second Chances
∽

It was under the endless blue skies of Phoenix, Arizona, that Carolynn and David first met. The year was 1964, they were both nineteen and they fell deeply in love. Carolynn Bauer was a stylish blond with a smile brighter than the desert sun bursting across her heart-shaped face. Dave was tall, his skin rosy, with horn-rimmed glasses resting on oversized ears, and brown hair shorn close to his head. In February he had begun boot camp in San Diego and was on leave to see his family and his girl. It was then that he proposed to Carolynn. Ecstatic, she said yes.

"It was a different time," Carolynn says now, "there was a real push for girls to get married young." It wasn't solely societal norms, however, that made her want to spend the rest of her life with Dave. "I may have been only nineteen, but I knew what I wanted. I was in love, I wanted to start a family, and I knew Dave would make a great father because he came from such a wonderful family." A date was set, their wedding was announced in the local paper, all was in place for a picture-perfect future when Dave, now a private first-class, heard rumors about his platoon going overseas. "The Marine Corps has such a history, such a tradition," he says.

"More than anything, I wanted to do a good job. I didn't want to be the weak link, the one who let the Marine Corps down."

It was then that he felt questions stirring deep inside of him. "Am I ready for marriage? What if I go overseas? Would it be fair to make Carolynn wait for me?" he asked himself, to which a voice inside him quietly replied, "No." Though he still wanted to marry Carolynn, he thought it would be better to wait until after his tour of duty.

Crushed, Carolynn ceased all communication with him, and though she kept in contact with his family, the topic of their shattered engagement was arduously avoided.

A storm had come through the desert city the night she finally placed a call to Camp Pendleton in San Diego. She stared out the window at the rain as she waited for the officer on duty to retrieve Dave from his barracks. She had no idea that he had completed infantry training, that it was his last night in America. The next morning, Dave was set to sail into what would become the Vietnam War. Thank God she had called. Carolynn asked him to reinstate their marriage plans, to step back into that picture-perfect future. "He still wanted to marry me," she says, "but not until he left the Marines." For Carolynn, that wasn't good enough. She wanted to set a date. "I thought I was the right age, that to wait until my twenties would be horrible." When he didn't change his mind, she put her foot down and gave him an ultimatum: marry her soon or lose her forever.

Carolynn returned the ring to Dave's mother the next day.

Around that time she was offered a job as a flight attendant with TWA. An exciting job for sure, but it required relocating to Chicago, a choice that seemed to make the dissolution of her relationship with Dave all the more permanent. But in her heart of hearts, Carolynn knew their union was meant to be. She sent him a letter that Dave received while aboard the USS *Pickaway*. He started to open it but changed his mind. Instead, he went about his duties on the ship, the mystery of the letter's contents weighing down his pocket. Was this the final kiss off? Had she officially decided to never see him again? Or did she want to reconcile their differences? He was a Marine, had just turned twenty years old, he needed to focus, keep up his end of the bargain and do a good job. He was going into combat. Was that any way to begin a marriage? He knew he didn't want any emotional ties, but he also didn't want to know if it was really over. When the torture became too much, he went on deck at sunset and stood at the edge of the ship. Dave took the unopened letter out of his pocket and hurled it overboard. The wind, however, blew it right back at him. How could he, a Marine, try to dispose of something against the wind? "I can't even throw a letter away!" he grumbled. There was a light rain that afternoon and the windswept envelope stuck neatly to the wet deck. Once he peeled it off the slick surface, the address began to bleed. Ink stained his fingers.

Annoyed at his mistake and determined to get rid of the letter and all the confusion it was causing him, Dave promptly marched to the tail of the ship and tossed it once again. This time, it fluttered in the wind for a few moments before landing in the Pacific, where it was churned in the ship's wake.

"I wish I could remember what it said," Carolynn laments. "I'm sure I asked him to reconsider or told him I would wait for him. I must have told him about the airline job. But that was over thirty-five years ago. I truly have no idea what it said." What she does remember was the fact she never received a reply. "I never wrote to him again." Carolynn moved to Chicago soon thereafter.

When Dave returned from Vietnam, he asked about Carolynn. She was married, he was told, and living in the Midwest. And though his mother occasionally wrote to her, Dave and Carolynn would not be in contact again until 1995, thirty-one years later.

That week in 1995 began typically enough: Carolynn's teenage son forgot to give her a message. "Oh yeah, someone named Dave called for you the other day." Dave? Did she know a Dave in Michigan, where she was then living? A few days later, he left another message, still with no last name. On his third attempt to reach her, Carolynn answered the phone. "This is Dave," said the voice on the other end of the line. "Dave who?" she asked. "Dave Zorn." "Dave Zorn," she repeated then wasted no time going right to the heart of the matter. "Why did you break up with me?" She asked because in her mind, by not answering her letter, he had abandoned her. Before he could answer she added, "I've never gotten over it."

In those intervening years a lot had happened. Carolynn had moved from Chicago to Seattle and finally settled in Detroit. She was now a mother of four. She had also been married three times. "I never believed in 'living with' someone without being married," she explains. For his part, Dave was the father of one son and, as with Carolynn, a lasting union had proved elusive: he was in the process of going through his second divorce. "I had never forgotten Carolynn," he says. "I got in touch with her because, with my divorce on the horizon, I figured it was now or never." They talked on the phone that day and the day after that. "It felt as if we hadn't spent a day apart," she says. It wasn't long before

Dave asked Carolynn to marry him. For the second time in her life, she told him yes.

This is the letter she read to him the night before their wedding. In it, not only does Carolynn make promises, she also states what she expects from him as a husband. "After several marriages each," she says, "we had learned what a marriage should and should not be. We knew, after being reunited, that we had picked the right partner many years ago."

I take you, David Richard Zorn, to be my husband, in every way. I promise to love you, to be faithful to you, to care for you in sickness and to share all that life will bestow upon us, be it tragedies or blessings, until death parts us temporarily. I also promise to be kind to you, to be a good companion and a joyful partner in life. I pledge to share my body with you willingly and happily as God intended when he created marriage. My desire is to not hinder you in any way from being the best man, the best father, the best employee, the best brother, the best son, the best husband, and the best human being you can and want to be. I want you to love and deeply care for me, protect me, nurture me, be kind to me,

*and insure that our home is a safe, quiet, and
loving place for ourselves and our families to
enjoy. I pray that God will bless this marriage
by granting us many years to enjoy each other
and to praise His name.*

Carolynn

183
•

It's been five years since she wrote those words to
her groom. And though they are happy together, with
Carolynn working as a writer and Dave as a radio news
anchor, there have been moments of sadness she compares to mourning. "We had lost so many years, so many
experiences," she says from her southern California home.
"We didn't grow up together, we'll never have kids
together. There have been times when it felt as if we
were grieving for the life we didn't have, for the memories we didn't create. There was definitely a period where
we were in mourning for lost years."

To see Carolynn and Dave, you would never guess
the history they share. Carolynn's smile is vibrant as
ever, and Dave has grown into his ears. Content, comfortable, affectionate partners in life, they are beginning
to recognize that there is no way of knowing how their
lives might have turned out if they had married in 1964.
The truth of their lives lies not in their past but in the
fact that they are here to love each other now.

A love letter can be inclusive, taking into account not just tender feelings for the central person in your life, but extending that love to include all those who matter to you both. That can be a very important kind of letter to write when the two central figures are heading the kind of "amalgamated" family that has become so common in recent decades. True love—at least for those who have passed beyond the close-up intensity of first love—can have a marvelously wide focus.

Completing the Picture

Mike, Kristi, and Marla sat at a table in a Mexican restaurant, sipping margaritas and chatting. It had been Marla's idea to bring them all together. For months Kristi had listened as Marla talked about her wonderful brother Mike. No doubt about it, Mike was nice looking, funny, and smart. He was miles more polite than the men Kristi had dated in the past. Even though they were getting along, one thing loomed in the back of her mind. He had sole custody of his three kids. Kristi was twenty-seven at the time and the idea of dating a person with so much responsibility was daunting. Especially since she had a six-year-old son of her own to think about. *Yes, he's a great guy*, she thought as a steaming plate of beans and rice was placed before her, *but I don't know . . .*

Mike and his ex-wife had grown up in the same small town in Nebraska. They dated for five years before they married; he thought they'd had a solid relationship and family. Over the ten-year span of their marriage, his wife became more and more flippant about the life they'd created together. When divorce became the only option, it was as if she'd felt no obligation to their children at all. She lived nearby but her visits were sporadic.

Eventually, even those visits ceased. With or without her, Mike refused to let his family down. He didn't have time to coach little league sports like other dads, but he did everything he could, from taking the kids to the movies to attending triple-A baseball games. Not one decision was made without the children's needs coming first. When he was offered a promotion to management—a position that called for frequent travel—he told his boss he needed time to think about it then checked with his parents and siblings. Sure, the job would bring in more money, but he would have turned it down if it meant less attention for his kids. A schedule was worked out with his family and the kids never did without care from a loved one.

Mike's capacity as a father was paralleled by Kristi's loyalty to her son, Kohlman. Unlike Mike, she had never been married. Her ex-boyfriend left town when she was in her second month of pregnancy, telling her his budding career as a professional football player was more important than starting a family. Still wanting to keep him informed, she called him as the due date neared. He, on the other hand, did everything in his power to avoid her calls. Even without him, Kristi had never been alone. She had raised her son with the loving support of her parents, who lived nearby. Disappointed but not bitter, Kristi would occasionally send photos of their son to her ex-boyfriend. She had a good job as an accounts manager at a trucking company and wasn't in need of child support. More than anything, she wanted to share the beauty of what they'd created. She wrote inviting him for a visit. He never responded.

Mike and Kristi's experiences as single parents did give them something in common, yet sitting in the Mexican restaurant that first night, she was apprehensive. Between work and family, they both were in high demand. There wasn't all that much room in either of their lives for casual dating and the idea scared her. Here was a guy she wanted to know better, yet the same two words churned through her head over and over: three kids. The following weekend Mike called and asked to see her again. Still uncertain about where any of this was going, she accepted. The two dined alone that evening and found they had much to talk about. Working for a trucking firm, Kristi's weekdays were spent in the presence of a lot of men—some of whom didn't take her seriously. With her petite frame, shiny red hair, and relaxed attitude she certainly wasn't the man they felt should have had her job. Over the years, Kristi had definitely learned to hold her own. Now here she was with Mike, relaxed and enjoying herself more than she had in years.

On the drive home, Kristi thought about what she

was getting herself into. Two of Mike's kids were older than Kohlman. They were going through stages of development she hadn't gone through with her own son. She imagined all the possible scenarios of introducing herself and Kohlman to Mike's family, finally realizing there was only one way to find out. She took a deep breath and began the next phase of her life.

The next weekend, Kristi picked up Kohlman from her parents' home and drove from Sioux City to Omaha. There, the four Schultes greeted them. With his dark blond hair and slender face, Mike's ten-year-old son Nick was the spitting image of his father. Only eight years old, Nathan already had a propensity for computers. He enthusiastically helped Kohlman reach the next level on a video game. Mike's daughter Tiffany, six, was well mannered and sweet, but couldn't be bothered with the boys. After dinner was over, she promptly excused herself and trotted over to her best friend's house next door.

Throughout the evening, Mike and Kristi sat stiffly in their chairs, anticipating jealousies among the kids or worse, a resentful attitude toward the adults. Nick had been second in command since his mother had moved out a few years before. Kristi couldn't help but think that of all the kids, he would be the one to give her a hard time. For all Mike and Kristi's apprehensions, the kids got along. They played together all night and were sad when it was time for Kohlman and his mom to go home. Now that they'd successfully crossed that bridge, Kristi and Mike kissed goodnight. They knew they'd be seeing a lot more of each other.

Though quiet by nature, Mike was never shy when it came to romance. Every weekend, Kristi and Kohlman drove to the Schultes' home. Once the kids were asleep, Mike always had something special planned just for the two of them. "Give me a half an hour," Mike said one Friday night as he stepped outside. Kristi sat patiently in the living room until he called her. She walked outside to find Mike standing on the deck bathed in candlelight, a hammock swinging gently in the breeze. "I thought we could watch the stars," he said, uncorking a bottle of Chardonnay. Kristi was beside herself with joy. She took a seat on the hammock only to have it instantly sink to the ground. Kristi couldn't help but laugh as Mike scrambled to help her up, apologizing profusely. He tightened the hammock ropes tethered to the porch supports. "Better?" he asked her as she sat on the cotton netting once again. "Better," she confirmed. The couple eased into the hammock. Mike wrapped his arm around Kristi's shoulders as they directed their gaze to the heavens above. Between her experience with Kohlman's dad and the occasional dates that always led nowhere, she never imagined a relationship could be like this. She playfully rubbed her nose against the softness of Mike's neck, content with everything around her. The hammock creaked. "Did you hear that?" Kristi managed to ask before the hammock gave way and they thumped to the ground, their flailing legs and arms knocking over lit candles and the open bottle of wine. Kristi laughed hysterically as Mike stomped away, his intimate evening ruined by an old hammock he hadn't used in years. They cleaned up the mess, though Mike still had a wrinkle in his brow. Once order was restored, they took a seat on the stairs instead. Kristi wrapped her arms around Mike's waist. He dropped his cheek on her head. The stars were just as beautiful from there.

After a month of seeing each other, Mike's kids began to call Kristi "mom." Why wouldn't they? She was concerned about their grades in school, she made their father happy, she and Kohlman were there every weekend to go to the movies and a baseball game. As far as Mike's kids were concerned, the six of them had become a family. Kristi gently explained to them that she had grown to love them just as she had grown to love their dad, but the simple truth was they had a mother. Their attachment to their "other mom," as the kids had begun to refer to their birth mother, was only biological. Kristi was the one they loved. She didn't want to dismiss their feelings for her, but she also didn't want to replace the natural connection between them and their mother.

When Mike occasionally spoke to the kids' mother, he never mentioned the fact that she hadn't come to visit for ages or that their divorce agreement stated she was supposed to pay child support. He knew the prevailing attitudes when it came to custody. Judges preferred to place children with their mothers, regardless of who was the better parent. What if the judge changed his mind? For years his ex-wife's behavior had been less than model but fear of losing his children kept Mike mum.

When strolling in the mall one afternoon, Mike suggested they pop into the jewelry store. "Let's just take a look," he said casually. It had only been three months since their first date at the Mexican restaurant and here they were, window-shopping for rings. Kristi peered over the glass cases, eyeing the rings that could fit their budget. "What about these over here?" he asked. "We can't afford those!" she said playfully, not even bothering to look. She was being prudent, but nothing could contain Kristi's excitement. Mike was going to propose! The only question was when.

A few weeks later, Mike did what had become their standard weekend practice: he prepared a special evening for the two of them after the kids had gone to bed. The fireplace was lit, a country ballad played softly from the stereo. Mike got down on one knee and took Kristi's hand into his. "I love you," he began, "and I love Kohlman. I want to spend the rest of my life with both of you. Will you be my wife?" he asked, tears rolling down his face. Kristi said yes, trying her hardest not to cry. It may have seemed like a short courtship to some, but the two of them knew their relationship was destined to work. He slid the ring on her finger. To Kristi's surprise, Mike had purchased a ring with eighteen diamonds. It must have come from the other side of the jewelry store, one of the expensive rings at which she had not even dared to look. Once the ring was secured on her finger, the precious stones glistening in the firelight, he handed Kristi the following letter. In it, he explained that his love was not just a romantic love but a holistic love encompassing him, her, and their four children.

3/28/96

My Dearest Kristi,

> *On this night I ask your hand in marriage, something I once told myself would not happen again. Before I met you I was convinced there was no one who could love*

me the way you do. I had all but resigned myself to the fact that I would be alone. What have I done to deserve someone like you is a question I ask myself often.

We are two pieces of a six-piece puzzle. I believe we fit together so perfectly and naturally that it is no wonder people can see the love we have for each other.

To have someone as special as you reaffirms my faith in God, for it is only he who could have created a person like you for me. Never have I known that there was someone whom I could love so completely and who could make me feel so completely loved—but you have. You make me so happy that I sometimes feel I have no right to be this happy.

You have become part of my heart, part of my soul, part of me. I want you to know that you can always count on me for comfort, love, and support for the rest of my life, through good times and difficult times. I will always be here for you and our kids.

I believe we have a once-in-a-lifetime

195
◆

*love; one all people dream of but very few
actually find.*

*On this night you have fulfilled my
dream!*

I love you more than these words can say,

196

Mike

Kristi could no longer contain herself. They held each other in front of the fireplace and wept tears of joy. Six months later they married, just the two of them, on the island of Antigua.

In the four years since Kristi and Mike wed, the Schultes have become the family they always desired, the family each of them deserved. Soon after the wedding, Kristi's parents invited each child individually to their home in Sioux City for special visits—a practice they continue to do to this day. It took a while for Nick to relinquish his position as second in command at the Schulte house. Kristi sometimes thought he resented her for coming into their lives. Now, she's come to realize it's not her, but a temporary yet serious affliction that has taken over Nick: he is now a teenager.

Recently, Kohlman saw his biological father playing football on television. When Kristi pointed the fact out to him, the child looked at the screen for a moment then went on playing. Ask him who his dad is and he will tell you it's the guy who now coaches little league, the guy who leaves his mother little love notes in her coffee pot, the guy who brings home pizza when no one wants to cook: Mike.

Mike's first wife has since moved to another state and before she left asked Kristi if she would legally adopt Nick, Nathan, and Tiffany. Kristi did adopt the children and, at the same time, Mike adopted Kohlman. They've also been blessed with a new addition to their family, a little girl named Taelor. Never once have terms such as "stepsister" or "stepfather" found a way into their home. While each child is aware of which union brought forth their births, they have also learned it takes more than blood to make a family.

There are times when a letter becomes truly obligatory. But the fact that you *must* write it does not necessarily detract from its significance or its emotional truth. Such letters can even bring about fulfillment of a long quest for full understanding.

Remembering Why

"Why would you marry your partner again?" the group leader asked. She and her husband sat side by side on their sofa, surrounded by couples who had assembled in their living room for this month's meeting. "Let's take a few minutes to reflect upon this, write down your answers and we will rejoin and discuss." This question was posed to the members of Image, a support group for married couples in Milwaukee. Image, a branch of Marriage Encounters, meets once a month to discuss issues of family and marriage. The group encourages exploration and dialogue between the couples, helping them find ways to lead more fulfilling lives. Having been part of this group for several years, Dr. James Schieffer and his wife, Faye, approached their assignment with vigor. The couples dispersed into separate rooms within the house to talk privately. Once alone in the den, Faye looked at her husband and said, "When I met you, it seemed like déjà vu. I felt like I had been looking for you all my life. I knew I had to marry you then and I know I would need to marry you again today."

Faye had met her husband at the urging of his sister. The two women were coworkers and decided a double date would be the best way for Faye and Jim to get to know each other. They hit it off immediately. Jim was a thoughtful man of science. He was accustomed to keeping his feelings inside until he met Faye. It was to her that he opened up like he never had before. He shared with her his desire to help people through medicine, his secrets and his fears. Faye, an easygoing and talkative woman, was a natural match for the pensive Jim. Their personalities complemented each other: she speaking when he was quiet, he adding introspection to her conversation. After a courtship full of discovery, they married in July of 1968. The honeymoon, real and metaphorical, could not last forever.

Jim was in his junior year of medical school, on his way to a profession that would surely bring economic stability. But the early years were tough. Especially when Faye would look around at her friends, their nice clothes and beautifully decorated homes, she would sometimes have doubts about her life. Her friends' husbands had gone into business or real estate while her husband was still a student. Cultural values teach us that money is paramount to happiness. If that was true then she and Jim, with his long hours and meager salary, were not "happy." "I was caught up in what I should have," she says now, "and not what I *did* have."

It was Faye who first read about the weekend retreats known as Marriage Encounters. The newsletter of their church in Wisconsin had run a series of articles describing the program. Marriage Encounters placed emphasis on communication and sharing. The meetings were structured around a topic and discussion, after which the couples talked and wrote privately. One wasn't expected to share with the entire group, only with his or her partner. The teachings were a blend of Catholic spirituality and psychology and never relied on one person to lead. Rather, couples took turns leading the discussions. In this fashion, everyone was working toward the same goal. Faye was eager to give it a try; Jim was apprehensive. But a priest asked him to attend. Jim was elected to check the program out as a member of the adult education council of their church and a physician. Faye was ecstatic.

From that first weekend retreat and the hundreds of meetings they have taken part in since, Faye and Jim learned the essentials for a strong marriage: forgiveness, acceptance, respect. They have come to understand that feelings are neither right nor wrong, they just are. They worked on breaking out of the roles of "husband" and "wife," eliminating the pattern of behavior that caused their relationship to stagnate in the beginning. It has changed the way they see the world and each other. The weekend retreats and the monthly meetings have also given them the strength to handle obstacles when they arise. When their oldest daughter developed an eating disorder, they were able to cope without blame. When their younger daughter was diagnosed with epilepsy, Jim accepted the help of other doctors. Their entire outlook on life has changed. "I'm not junk," Faye says passionately. "I'm not a mistake. God doesn't make junk. Yes, we make mistakes but that doesn't mean we are the mistake. There's a reason why all of us are here."

And now, here they were at an Image meeting, after thirty-two years of marriage being asked why they'd do it all again. Faye and Jim leaned over their pads of paper and quietly wrote for ten minutes. Then, it was time to share.

Faye, My Beauty,

I would marry you on the tallest peak of the Rocky Mountains, so high do you make me feel.

I would marry you on the Queen Mary, *so royal do you make me feel.*

I would marry you on a starry night under the brilliance of aurora borealis, so heavenly do you make me feel.

I would marry you at the fireplace of our home, so warm do you make me feel.

*I would marry you at St. Francis Cathedral,
so full of faith do you make me feel.*

*I would marry you in our bed, so full of love
do you make me feel.*

*I would marry you in every way, my heart
always looking forward to all that we can
share.*

All my love, Jim

———————

My Dearest, Handsome Jim,

*We've been blessed with love from the
universe to keep us growing side by side. And
for this I would marry you again.*

*When I think of all we've gone through
over the years, it's mind-boggling we are still
together. I love how you have persevered at
work and I love how you have persisted with
me. I know I have been rough on you. My
spoiled demands, all my early expectations
that you should be a walking god—sacrificing
over and over to prove your undying love
for me.*

I hope I can give you more as the years

come in ways you need the most. You deserve far more than you get. From now on, I will not keep my love for you to myself. Teach me what you most need, what you most desire.

I love sleeping beside you every night, love gazing upon you when you sing in the choir, love falling in love with you over and over again.

Your beauty, Faye

Jim wrapped his arms around his wife. Faye rested her cheek upon his chest. They stood this way, giving all the love they could, until it was time to rejoin the group.

A Valentine letter must not be ordinary. It can be decorated to make it special, of course, or it can be presented with a gift, beautiful flowers, or a huge silken heart filled with chocolates. But there are even more imaginative ways to make a Valentine letter especially memorable.

Surprises

Four-year-old Savannah wanted to make this the best Valentine's Day ever because her daddy was simply the best! With the help of her mother, she took out a tablet of construction paper and went to work. From the red paper they made hearts and from the white paper they cut out doves. "Maybe we should hang them all over the house," her mother suggested. The girl's face lit up like the sun as her mother ran to grab the yarn. After all the ornaments were hung, they opened the window just a bit so the little paper hearts and doves flitted gently in the breeze. Now it was time for a picture. Savannah took out her crayons and began to draw with great care. When she was done, she showed it to her mommy. "That's you, that's Daddy, that's Cameron, and that's me!" This effervescent child had no idea how much her crayon family portrait would mean to her father. For if her parents had listened to their doctors, there would have been no family portrait at all.

"There are three things in Sullivan," Stephanie Ray Brown says of the small town in Kentucky where she and her husband were raised. "A barbecue, a stoplight, and a roller rink." Well, thank goodness for the roller rink! It was there that Stephanie first got acquainted with fifteen-year-old Terry Brown. All night she waited for this bashful boy to ask her to skate. He wobbled past her every now and again but couldn't work up the courage to say anything. So Stephanie did what any self-respecting fourteen-year-old girl would: she skated with his best friend. Eventually, Terry came up to her, his legs shaky in the lace-up boots. "I guess the next one's a couple's dance," he said. Stephanie understood exactly what Terry wasn't too good at saying. She clutched him and they skated around the rink hand in hand.

From then on, she and Terry were a team. When her mother refused to let her go out alone with a boy, they stuck it out through two years of supervised dates. Terry was on the basketball team and Stephanie was a cheerleader. When Terry went off to college a year before Stephanie finished high school, he remained faithful. She, in turn, applied to the same school. And it was at Murray State that the two became engaged. They married in 1980, after seven years of dating, but the true test of their partnership was still on the horizon.

After a year of trying, they were unable to conceive a baby. Eager to start a family, they went to a doctor who, after a series of tests, suggested adoption. Floored, they sought the help of a specialist. He explained how Stephanie was lucky to even ovulate. She turned to her husband, using her wit to hide her pain. "Great. So you're a stud and I'm a dud." But the situation was no laughing matter. They both wanted a child desperately, and Stephanie's confidence was beginning to falter. She tried to blame herself for their misfortunes, but Terry wouldn't let her. They were, after all, a team. The next month, Stephanie was scheduled for in vitro fertilization. The day before the procedure, she was given a pregnancy test. And it came back positive. "You got my blood mixed up with somebody else's," she told the nurse, not at all amused. There hadn't been any mixup. She was pregnant with Savannah. Three years later, she gave birth to Cameron. "One was a blessing," she now says. "But two was a miracle!"

When Terry came home on Valentine's Day, he found the housed decked out in symbols of love. Doves, hearts, a candy-colored family portrait. Looking around their house only confirmed what he'd known all along: he was a lucky man. Then Savannah led her daddy on a treasure hunt. Terry went to the sofa and found a red heart. "Not here," the paper heart read. "Try the kitchen." Savannah giggled with delight. In the kitchen, Terry found another. "Keep looking. Maybe in the hall closet." Each paper heart led him closer to the card Savannah and Stephanie had made that afternoon. When he finally found the red-and-white creation, this is what he read:

I am so proud to say
the man I vowed to love to the very end

is not only my lover
but also my best friend.

It began in the small town of Sullivan
April 15 was our first date
when this soft-spoken guy
with big beautiful brown eyes
asked me to skate.

"I do not skate very well
as you can see . . .
but on next Couple's Skate
will you skate with me?"

We stayed sweethearts at Webster County High
became engaged at Murray State.
Now celebrating thirteen years of marriage
May 16 being our wedding date.

Married to this man
has been wonderful but not without its doubts
As far as children went
we had to learn to do without.

The doctors said, "Maybe
it just wasn't meant to be . . ."
However, they just didn't know
how much Terry loves me.

SURPRISES

At this time in our marriage
I tried to push him away.
I was the reason why we could not have children
so with me he should not have to stay.

"We both want children," he said.
"You know this is true.
We can always adopt children
but I can't adopt you!
If I was the one with the problem
you would not leave me.
So we'll get through this together.
It'll be okay, you'll see!"

For two years he kept my spirits high
he would not let me frown
Until June 7th our miracle arrived:
Savannah Ashley Brown.
But our family did not end here,
I am happy to say,
when three years later,
Cameron Michael came our way!

As we tuck our children in bed,
I realize doctors are smart.
However, they did underestimate
the power of the heart.

Whether it's my daughter
who has her dad's big beautiful brown eyes
or my son who has his dad's dimpled grin
Every time I look at them I fall in love again . . .

With that same big brown-eyed boy
who did not know how to skate.
But who knew just how to glide into my heart and
make my life great!

On our twentieth Valentine together
I would just like to say
I love you Terry Brown
on Valentine's
and every single day!

Savannah could tell her daddy was happy with all they did. He thanked them and then gave her and Cameron big, wet kisses. But he saved the biggest kiss for her mom.

All of us, whether we admit it or not, need to be rescued at some point in our lives. We have lost our way, and we cannot see well enough through the gloom of our circumstances or the fog that clouds our minds to make our way forward without a guiding hand. If such a hand does reach out to take hold of ours, the only way to fully express our gratitude and love may be in a letter of celebration and thanksgiving.

Healed by Love

All of Jenna's dreams revolved around the stage. She had begun studying acting and voice as a teen, performed in high school plays, had modeled in advertisements. She was a natural in the theater, comfortable in front of a camera. Her talents took her to Boston University, where she studied drama, matching her passion for performing with an equal amount of hard work. Not long after graduating, Jenna began touring the country with a children's theater group. She had attained so many of her goals at a young age when others were getting discouraged and giving up. So why was she suddenly having this anxious feeling every time she tried to leave her apartment? At first it was a mild tingle inside then slowly the feeling swelled. She would start breathing heavily, anxiety would set in sometimes to the point of feeling nauseated. Concerned, she consulted a physician. He found nothing wrong with her, but the feeling didn't subside. On the contrary, it intensified. She would get up in the morning and start the day as usual, but when it came time to start walking out the door, her heart would flutter. Some days it got so bad she would call in sick for rehearsal. Then she missed a few performances. Then she was out of a job.

A psychologist diagnosed the panic attacks as ago-raphobia (*agora* is the Greek word for open market squares), which is the fear of leaving one's house. It had gotten to the point where Jenna never wanted to leave the apartment. With no income, however, she couldn't stay there either. Her parents were supportive and urged her to come home. She refused, believing it was just a passing affliction. One afternoon, while both of her roommates were out at work, she went to the kitchen only to find the refrigerator empty. There was a conve-nience store around the corner. She would get a loaf of bread and a jar of peanut butter; that would be enough to last until her roommates came home. She went to the door and reached for the knob. Her heart raced, she felt dizzy and disoriented, her body began to tremble. *You can walk there*, she told herself. *It's one block away. You don't have to drive. You can do it.* With her hand on the doorknob she fell to her knees, shaking, in tears, and remained that way for two hours. She couldn't feed her-self. Jenna called her mother, who begged her to come home. Defeated, she moved back with her parents.

Agoraphobia strikes many women like Jenna: early to mid-twenties, college-educated, driven to succeed. Now the world as she knew it no longer existed. In the confines of her parents' home, acting was no longer an option. Her friends didn't understand where the Jenna they knew had gone. In the beginning, a few made the effort to drive from Boston to see her in upstate New York, but as the months went on, most of the visits stopped. Needing to support herself, she started looking into jobs she could do from home and was soon writing for a variety of on-line magazines. Working from her computer was fine, but it wasn't a cure. She wanted to get better but didn't know how. She saw several therapists, and tried a variety of medications, all of which made her nauseated and none of which helped.

One friend she could always count on was Sean, whom she had worked for back in high school. His band, Code Bleu, performed at small clubs and weddings, and Jenna had been their secretary. He visited her regularly, always trying to coax her out of the house. He even tried to set her up on a date. "I've hardly left the house in two years!" Jenna said, shocked Sean would even suggest such a thing. "Who wants to date someone who can't . . . date?" "He doesn't care about that," Sean insisted. Jenna couldn't believe it. What kind of guy wouldn't care?

She went to check her e-mail one afternoon and found a friendly message from Anthony. She was going to kill Sean! Jenna quickly typed, "Thanks for writing, but I'm not interested in meeting you." Anthony, however, continued to write. He played saxophone and guitar and liked every kind of music one could imagine: classical, country, reggae, rock, jazz. The band he played with did weddings on the weekends, but during the week he taught music at a private school.

After a few weeks, Jenna had the courage to write back. "I am no fun," she began. "I have had this condition for over two years and it's not going away." In that time, she'd managed to leave her home a handful of times for therapy visits, though often she preferred having her counseling sessions over the phone. One time her brain had been so thick with medication that she forgot how to tie her shoe. There were days when she lost large blocks of time just staring into space. She could not function.

"I just wanted to lay it on the line," she says now. "I had been an accomplished woman. I loved theater and comedy clubs and going dancing. I loved people. I was so different from who I really was and I hated it. I wanted him to meet *me*, not some shaking little girl."

She checked her computer, sure she had gotten rid of him. "Maybe we could practice just walking around the block," he replied.

Slowly, they worked up to talking on the phone— phone conversations that would last up to eight hours! One autumn evening as Jenna and Anthony talked on the phone, the clock struck midnight. From a place inside she still cannot describe, Jenna gathered every bit of courage she had and said, "Come over."

As soon as she hung up, she ran up the stairs and woke her sister. Having spent the last few years in sweatpants and T-shirts, she needed something to wear. Her sister ran to her mother's room. "Mom, wake up! Anthony's coming over!" Her mother and sister were ecstatic watching Jenna go through outfit after outfit. For the first time in years, she wanted to look cute, she wanted to look sexy, she wanted to brush her hair! Just as she put the final touches on her makeup, the doorbell rang. Jenna's anxiety set in. "Go answer it!" She pushed her mom toward the door then sprinted to the kitchen to hide. Jenna peeked around the corner. They had e-mailed each other pictures and she thought he was cute. Now that he was in her living room, his face framed by a halo of soft brown curls, she found him striking.

She crept out of the kitchen to embrace Anthony. Her mother and sister returned to bed while Jenna and Anthony settled on the couch. Sure, she was nervous. But she also felt alive. Without warning, the world and her place in it made sense again. Jenna was back.

As the day broke, they walked out of her front door. Jenna stood on the porch for a second and looked into Anthony's green eyes. *You can do this*, she told herself.

She took one step onto the sidewalk and then another and another. They made it to a nearby park and sat by a waterfall to watch the sunrise.

A year has passed since that day and they have just moved in together. "After five shrinks and six medications," Jenna now says, "all it took was Anthony walking through my front door!"

After having been so debilitated by fear, Jenna says the most important aspect of their relationship is their ability to have fun. In the letter below, she describes how together they find joy in everyday living.

Sir Anthony,

Sometimes, I wonder if you are at all aware of how many times you make me smile everyday.

When you left for work today, you turned on the computer for me and left Xs and Os on the screen, because you knew that would be the first place I'd go when I got up. You left a snack next to the keyboard because you knew I wouldn't stop to eat without a reminder. You pinned up our kindergarten school pictures right next to each other on the bulletin board

to remind me that we are each other's missing
childhood playmates.

I don't just feel lucky because you are the
most wonderful man I've ever known. I also
feel lucky because I don't know many other
adults who remember how to play. You
brought fun back into my life. You and your
guitar and your tackle hugs and your silly pet
names. Who knew that mundane everyday
tasks could be so much fun? We go shoe
shopping and it's an adventure. We go to the
grocery store and wind up slow dancing in the
dairy aisle. And the greatest part of it all is
that you think you're the lucky one!

I feel so understood, so free. I know that
no matter what I do, you won't look at me
funny. You'll join me. You'll one-up me. And
that will be our game. I could fill your
bathtub with rose petals and you would
stomp "I love you, Violetfairy" into the snow
outside my window as a reply.

I'm still in awe, everyday, that the
universe fell into alignment long enough to let
us meet. Blind dates are supposed to be

223
•

traumatic. They aren't supposed to last ten hours, ending up at a park at sunrise. You noticed that I was carrying my pocketbook in one hand and my water bottle in the other as we walked along the lake. You knew it was because I was afraid to hold your hand. When we sat down by the waterfall, you asked me for a hug instead of a kiss.

224
❖

I kissed you. I couldn't help it. You were so damn cute.

Today, before you left for work, I woke up just long enough to kiss you again.

I still can't help it. You've gotten even cuter.

You didn't even flinch at my morning breath. Now that's *love.*

I want to thank you for a thousand things. For paying attention. For not letting me hide from love. For making every lonely day before we met seem completely inconsequential. For being on my team. For having the guts to keep bugging me until I agreed to bind and gag my fears long enough to meet you in person. And mostly, for being the love of my life.

You aren't the man of my dreams . . . my dreams were never this good! I didn't dare to hope for you, because I didn't believe you existed. I hope I can bring you the kind of joy you give me every day, and I hope you're smiling one of your big warm smiles right now.

Loving you,
Violetfairy

What could be better than letters from a songwriter? Perhaps only
the letters from the person who is the wellspring
for those songs.

Chance Meeting

Like so many young people in the 1960s, seventeen-year-old Linda Friedman and her sister Cheryl were itching to explore the world. With not much more than a few pieces of clothing shoved in a backpack, they took off for Europe in the spring of 1969 determined to soak up the sights and sounds of each country like rays from the sun. They were looking for adventure, not romance, but of course anything could happen. Traveling quickly brought younger sister Linda out of her shell. They met so many different people on their journey across the Continent that by the time they got to the fairy-tale city of Copenhagen, Denmark, the formerly shy Linda could strike up a conversation with just about anyone. As soon as they checked into the girls' dormitory of a youth hostel, Linda went downstairs to take a look around the cafe to see who was there.

Sitting by the window was a guy of about her age with long, curly brown hair and ripped jeans. A guitar case lay at his feet. He was the only person in the place by himself so she walked straight up to him and said, "Hi, my name's Linda, what's yours?" He was Richie Pollock of Brooklyn, New York. At that point, Richie had been traveling for a few months. He and his buddy Fred had gotten to Europe the cheapest way they could think of: on a Yugoslavian freighter. After seven rocky days at sea, he and Fred docked in Algeria then hopped a ferry into Spain, took a train through France, and eventually wound up in Copenhagen.

Richie enjoyed opening up to strangers, though it seemed everyone he met was from New York. It was nice to meet kids with experiences similar to his, but he'd come a long way, had sold records, headphones, clothes, and anything else he could think of in order to get *away* from New Yorkers. Now that he was here, home just seemed to follow him.

"So, where are you from?" he asked with a sigh, expecting this Linda person to answer Long Island, Brooklyn, or perhaps Queens.

"Montreal," she said with a smile.

Richie straightened up in his chair.

"Do you play?" she asked, pointing to the guitar case.

Richie had been playing only a short while but was already writing songs. On the long trip over from the United States, he'd finished his first song, now he was on his second. "It's called 'Europe on $5 a Day,'" he said with a laugh.

Linda was studying to be a piano teacher for young children. It turned out both she and Richie loved going wild to acid rock, but it was the quiet strength of folk music that touched their souls. Joni Mitchell, Bob Dylan, Ramblin' Jack Elliott—those were their heroes. They were soon joined by Linda's sister Cheryl, and then by Richie's friend Fred. Hours of conversation just flew by.

The guys had stayed in an amazing hotel before winding up in the dumpy youth hostel. Richie described the Hotel Knudsen as if he'd discovered Shangri-La. "Five windows and a view of the square . . . ," Richie said with solemn reverence. They'd only been able to stay there for a few nights before the management told them the room had been promised to others. It was a drag to be sharing a dorm room for the same price. Needless to say, the boys were looking to get out of the youth hostel as soon as possible.

Neither Richie nor Fred had ever seen a moped until they arrived in France. As soon as they realized they didn't even need a driver's license to purchase one, they cashed in their rail passes and bought two of the little scooters to buzz around the Continent. Since they had been in Denmark a few days, the guys offered to take Linda and Cheryl on a tour of the city the next morning. That night Linda sat in her bed, furiously scribbling in her journal. She recounted all the wonderful things about Richie ending with the words, "One day I hope to marry someone just like him!"

231
◆

Over the next five days, they went to Tivoli Gardens and the Carlsburg brewery, they strolled the famous Walking Street where no cars were permitted, allowing locals and tourists alike to do their shopping free of traffic. Linda and Richie shared a bag of fresh peas that they popped in their mouths straight from the pod. As the peas exploded on her tongue, Linda was sure she had never tasted anything so sweet! They discovered a record store where customers could listen to an entire album on headphones before purchasing it. And every night came to a close with Richie strumming his guitar in the youth hostel cafe, his heartfelt lyrics and passionate singing sending warmth through the room. Linda admired Richie's natural ability and, when she looked around the room at the faces enraptured by his performance, she knew she wasn't the only one touched by his gift.

At the various places she and Cheryl had stayed in, the other students were into talking about how hopeless and awful the world was. To Linda, that grim outlook on life somehow seemed practiced; as if it was what they thought they *should* be saying instead of what they really felt. With Richie it was different. Over those five days in Denmark she had come to know a true and honest person. He had a looping, playful way of speaking, the notes of his voice jumping up and down with excitement. His face became alive and animated whether he was talking about bullfights he'd seen in Spain or his mother back in Brooklyn. Often he'd get so caught up in what he was saying he'd trip over his own feet or bump into a wall. His clumsiness was just one more thing that made her smile. He was generous with compliments, unpretentious by nature, and seemed unbelievably happy. They had discovered a valuable friendship, but their time together was quickly coming to an end.

233
◆

On the sisters' last night in Denmark, they joined Richie and Fred at the popular Club 27. An oil-and-water projection graced the walls with ever-changing psychedelic designs while Jefferson Airplane songs wailed from the speakers. Richie knew he might not ever see Linda again. He'd wanted to kiss her since the first day she boldly introduced herself at the cafe, and now it was do or die. He lifted his arm, gingerly attempting to wrap it around her shoulder. Just as his arm was about to drop, Linda leaned a bit forward. With his arm still outstretched, he moved toward her again and once more, Linda leaned forward just out of his reach. He liked her and he thought she liked him, but Richie wasn't into playing cutesy, flirtatious games. He excused himself and joined another group of people he knew.

In fact, Linda hadn't been flirting at all. Much the

opposite, his advances had turned her back into the same shy girl from Montreal she'd always been. Regardless, he was ready to call it a night. Richie and Fred had moved into a new hotel by that point and he would have left without so much as a good-bye except his coat was sitting on the chair beside Linda. When he returned to the table, Linda scooped up his hands in hers and looked deep into his eyes. The last five days had been positively joyous. She knew she'd found her other half and there was no way she would let it end like this. "Pick me up tomorrow morning," she said.

The next morning he drove her to the train station on his moped. They stood between the train cars, whispering good-byes. He leaned toward her and gave her a kiss: their first kiss and quite possibly their last. Linda couldn't believe the dizziness she felt from his lips. Everything about him made her feel tingly and alive. Just then, the train violently jerked forward causing Richie to whack his head against the door. Linda screamed with laughter as the ever-clumsy Richie tumbled down the stairs of the moving train and fell onto the platform. On his knees, he waved good-bye.

Two days after returning home to Montreal, as Linda sat on her bed towel-drying her hair, she wondered if she would see her lovely, clumsy Richie ever again. At that moment, she heard the mail slip through the slot in the door. Amid the envelopes addressed to her parents was one for her—from Richie.

September 5th, 1969

Dear Linda,

Today makes my fifth month in the wide world and Fred and I have already been on our island for almost a week. I certainly hope you enjoyed your travel (I really hope you hated every minute of it because I wasn't there) and gained much knowledge and experience. As for myself, I remain my dull, clumsy (remember our farewell on the train from Copenhagen) but lovable self.

By the way, I certainly hope you remember me and you're not reading this letter in complete bewilderment as to who it's from. It is I, Richard Pollock, the dashing fellow you so easily charmed in Copenhagen, that glorious city. I can't even tell you how many times I've thought of you in the month and a half since I saw you last. The first couple of weeks you were constantly on my mind and then as time progressed you came to mind when I was feeling down or simply pensive. I certainly hope my memory has not dimmed from your mind. But if it has, you can be sure when I get back to New York you will receive a call from me and I will ignite your memory even if I have to set fire to the phone to do it.

How's Cheryl? Did the two of you have a good rest in Switzerland? Are you even home now? Are you going to answer this letter? I certainly hope you do because all I have to remember you by is what I wrote in my log and a picture Fred took of you, Cheryl, and me. I'd love to read a letter from you to assure me you're still alive and also that you still care enough to keep up what was our so transient relationship in Copenhagen. Really, please answer. Aw, come on, you know you can't resist me!

Love,
Richie

Linda couldn't believe it. She was thinking of him, and his letter appeared. Just like their chance meeting, it seemed as if the universe was guiding them toward each other. She excitedly answered his letter the next day.

September 15, 1969

Dear Richie,

237

I can't tell you how happy I was to hear from you! Just the night before, when I came home from Paris, I was telling my sister how much I hoped to receive a letter from you. When I did the next morning, I went absolutely out of my mind. For about fifteen minutes I was just sitting there, staring at the envelope, smiling, laughing—I couldn't even open it. I was just so glad that you actually wrote. And after I read it I was twice as happy.

How could you possibly even think that I could forget who you are? Never. I bet you thought that after I left you I never thought about you at all. God, are you ever wrong! After I left you it seemed like my trip was getting better and better and I really did gain

*much knowledge and experience. I met so
many fabulous people and saw so many great
things yet I thought about you often. I am so
happy that you thought about me also. Say
hello to Fred for me. You've got to tell me all
about that wonderful island you're living on
and what you do there. By the way, your
memory has not dimmed from my mind at
all, but I'd still love for you to call me so I can
actually speak to you. It'll be thrilling but
funny to hear your voice after such a long
time (although I remember it exactly).*

Linda went on to tell Richie about the rest of her
time in Europe and then signed off with an invitation to
continue writing.

*It's just so wonderful having a true friend like
you because the people around here are so
phony. You're a real person and you proved it
when you popped right out of those pages you
wrote me. It's time to say so long so that you
can write me back right away.*

Love,
Linda

December 1, 1969

Dear Linda,

 It is snowing at the moment, the big flakes are swirling in the wind and landing here and there to either join with other flakes in a conglomerate or else to fall alone on the barren sidewalk and melt into a meaningless trickle of water in the last expansive sea of wet pavement. And needless to say, I am safe and warm in my own little cubicle listening to some recently purchased albums on my lousy record player.

 Also, in this same instant of time, you are here on my mind. My thoughts are going back to a pleasant day in late November, in fact it was a Wednesday, it was my birthday. I recall going down to my mailbox and being greeted with an extremely pleasant birthday present in the form of your letter. In the two or so weeks that lapsed in our communication link, I was starting to have my doubts about your end, but all doubts were instantly dispelled at the sight of your lovely scrawl on the envelope.

*You my dear friend are a truly wonderful
person and I mean that in all sincerity.*

*I am a Sagittarius, with my heart ruled
by my head, according to my right palm. I
grew up uneventfully except for the fact that I
had to do this without a father. My parents
were divorced when I was about a year old so
I have no memory of my father and
consequently have no idea of what I missed by
having no idea of what I had or didn't have as
the case may be.*

*Have I told you about our trip home?
From Livorno, Italy, we caught ourselves
another Yugoslav freighter and the trip back
took two weeks. During that time there was a
storm in the Atlantic in which two vessels
sunk. Needless to say, we got our share of
tossing and turning, not to mention
seasickness. But we made it to New York in
one piece and after a week or two home, my
mother started pestering me to get a job. So I
got myself a haircut (out of necessity, but it
turned out beautifully) and after a couple of
days, I found a job. I'm doing manual labor*

and some inventory for a record distribution company.

I've been writing songs lately, actually my brother has been giving me lyrics of his and I've been writing tunes to them on my nifty twelve-string guitar. About that song I wrote to you . . . I figure the reason I can't get a suitable tune to it is because the subject is too close to me, if you know what I mean. I was meaning to start off this letter with a quote from the song. Since I didn't do it then I may as well do it now:

When I saw you I was unaware
That you would be the one
That could do what had never been done.
With your long brown hair
As you sat in the chair
And you innocently stepped into my life.

Linda, I deeply appreciate your feelings toward me and I can only say that I'm really honored that you can fall into that sacred category of "friend." You, my dear Linda, fall into

my category of one of the sweetest, most sin-
cere, beautiful girls I have ever met and
because of my encounter with you, Copen-
hagen will forever be implanted in my mem-
ory as the best place in the world. You are a
shining star in my constellation of friends and
I hope we can always keep in touch even if we
can't see each other as often as we'd both like.
I know for myself that I'd like to see you
everyday, but such things are impossible, sad
to say.

Love,
Richie

Richie's letters were a bright spot in Linda's life; a life that, after seeing the sights of Europe, now seemed dull. She wanted to return to friendly people and funny little houses. She was ready for more village walks, pungent cheese, and fresh peas. She wanted the freedom of having everything she needed strapped to her back. Though it had only been a year, she booked another flight to Europe and, just as it had before, fate nudged her toward Richie. Her flight had a stopover in New York. By then he had moved from Brooklyn to the heart of the folk music scene in Greenwich Village. He had been hanging out with poets and painters, but never had Richie seen such an amazing sight as Linda's slim figure gracing his doorway. Her wavy hair spilled down her shoulders to the small of her back, the chains of her belt gently clinking around her hips with every step she took toward him. They spent that evening together and then, once again, Linda launched across the sky.

As she hitched around the Continent, the time to write Richie became scarce. One part of her wanted to backpack around Europe forever; yet, without Richie by her side, the peas didn't taste nearly as sweet. Upon returning home, she promptly called him. She would invite him to Montreal. Somehow she could work it out with her parents. Maybe he could stay in the guest room or at one of her friends' houses. Oh, how happy she was to be talking with him again! It had been a long time but Linda hadn't realized how long until Richie mentioned he'd been seeing someone else. Linda sat in a daze, the phone pressed against her ear. Had she heard him correctly? "Did you say," she ventured, "nine months? You've been going with her nine months?"

After a rushed good-bye, Linda put down the phone. She was crushed. She'd waited too long and now he was in love with someone else. She would never have called him back if it weren't for her sister Cheryl. Cheryl

243

had seen the two of them together in Copenhagen and noticed the magic they created in each other's presence. "Invite him anyway," she urged. Linda called him back and before the words were halfway out of her mouth, he accepted.

Linda and her mother went to the airport to meet him. When Mrs. Friedman saw her daughter run up to a long-haired young man wearing an embroidered vest and no shirt underneath, she was just a tad bit surprised. "I was supposed to marry a wealthy accountant or lawyer," Linda says now of her mother's expectations. "And here comes this guy off the airplane carrying a paper bag with nothing but a shirt and a demo tape in it. On the way to the car, my mother whispered, 'Where's his change of underwear?'"

For two more years they communicated by letters and phone calls, refusing to let geography stand in the way.

February 26, 1972

My Dear Love,

This whole year has been constant waiting for us. Waiting for each phone call, each letter, each possible weekend or holiday to be together. I can't wait until I'm with you when time no longer exists, waiting no longer exists.

So, I'm moving to New York City! It may be the jungle of dirt, but it's still an exciting, important step in my life. I'll have left home for good, out on my own, making my own decisions, being independent, growing up, learning and experiencing so much. Another interesting chapter in the life of Linda Friedman. It's a major turning point and I'm proud of myself for knowing what I want and going right out and doing it. Three cheers for Linda!

Everyone says beware of New York. I know there is justification for saying that, but to me it's fun. It's a study of people, for New York, like every city, tells a story. I'm not afraid. It's the capital of the world and I'm out to investigate!

It's also a fine cultural center and us cultural folks must take advantage of it. There's so much going on there; new, experimental things happening all the time.

245
❖

*And so much of it is free! Leave it up to me to
find out about it all. We'll make it fun—us,
together.*

*And what a rewarding experience it will
be for us to live with each other! To care,
share, and compromise; another step in our
knowledge about life. You are the person I
admire and respect above all persons, the one
I truly want. Wow, I've got everything! I'm so
lucky. Just thinking about you makes me
quiver because more than my love for you, I
feel truly honored that you have chosen me to
hold your hand through our lifetime. I must
say, it's not a bad choice. I think you've made
a wise decision.*

*And so, what have I got to complain
about? Still, I miss you. Love is the most
powerful thing in the world! You have made
me so optimistic, fearless, ready for anything
as long as we are together. I'm going to
Florida with my parents and then straight to
your arms!*

*My soul cries to join yours forever in
union for, as you know, we shall be all the*

246
◆

more complete when finally our bodies are
resting together as intended, as planned, as
must be.

> *I adore you,*
> *Linda*

247
❖

Linda was correct when she wrote "forever in union." One afternoon, while riding in the back of a taxicab, Richie asked Linda, "So, do you want to get married?"

They had a large wedding in Montreal, and then flew to Copenhagen to celebrate their union in the charming city where their love was born. They stayed in the very room overlooking the square that Richie had had when he first visited Copenhagen in the summer of 1969 and met a girl who wasn't from New York.

Some letters come to be treasured not for their passion nor because
they are reminders of a time of special significance.
They are treasured instead for their very ordinari-
ness, for the fact that they reflect the quiet joys of
day-to-day life as it is lived with a loved one. They
take on a significance beyond what they say. And
they can be quite short and still speak volumes.

Simple Pleasures

Since Flora La Bar's husband Bart passed away in 1995, she has been giving away many of his books. This is not because they were a painful reminder of how much she has lost, but because it's what Bart wanted her to do. "I donated writing books to the senior center, which has a writing class, history books to a local reading group, about eight boxes of books on photography to the high school, and maybe another twelve boxes on all sorts of topics to the library." Many organizations can be thankful for Bart's endless appetite for knowledge.

Bart was a voracious reader. "He bought books all the time," Flora says. "He liked going to auctions where you bid a couple of dollars on a box sight unseen. It was a sort of a hobby of his." Bart was particularly interested in books about birds, photography, and the history of the Old West. "The local waitresses called him 'Professor' because there were so many subjects about which he would just pull facts and figures out of his head. He could talk for hours on a subject if it interested him." Flora remembers with amusement that Bart sometimes knew more about a particular law of the Old West or about the life of a noted cowboy than the curators of the western history museums they visited. And to put the cap on the extent of his interests, Flora adds, "He read the almanac for pleasure."

Bart was a trained psychiatric nurse. "I'm the one with the MBA," Flora says, "but I think he was more educated." But she loved to read, too, although they had different interests. "I like inspirational books, how-to books, or fiction. Lately, I've been reading a lot of books about funny female detectives. I like to be entertained." During their twenty-three years of marriage, they would provoke comments in restaurants. People would wonder if they even knew each other. "We'd be sitting there, not talking, just reading away. But that was our interest, that's what we liked to do."

There is a letter Flora particularly treasures, because it says so much about their lives. It was no more than a note really, but it encompasses a great deal.

February 5, 1982

My Dear Sweet Bride—

A note to tell you that I love you more today than the day we married. Your beauty is more vibrant to me now than when we wed. And as each day, month, year passes, your beauty and my love for you grows.

I truly hope you will forgive me for my minor transgressions, such as buying 215 paperback books. There really are some good ones in this batch.

Love and kisses,
Bart

Flora has given away a great many of Bart's books, as he wanted. But there are plenty left, more than any one person needs, Flora says. "And, yes, there are some good ones in my batch, too."

A wedding brings an exchange of vows, and for most people that is all that is necessary to put the seal on their shared love and the promises that fill their hearts. But the wedding vows are formal in nature, part of a ritual, and there are those who feel the need to say something further, something more personal. The additional words may be hard to say aloud in the emotional atmosphere of a wedding day without choking up a little. A letter, a very special letter that can be preserved and cherished by the couple through the years, may be the perfect solution.

Expressions of Love

They played the violin.

He was sixteen, she only fifteen, but they saw each other regularly at the rehearsals of the Greendale, Wisconsin, high school orchestra in the late 1970s. They tucked their violins up under their chins, and they brought their bows down across the strings and tried to make beautiful music. Of course, it was only a high school orchestra, and there were inevitably some wrong notes here and there. But August Ray and Geralee Brown had no difficulty recognizing that there was some kind of special music in the air between them. Within one month of starting to date, they were certain they were destined to marry.

They were romantic kids, but they also had a sense of humor. Ask Augie what first sparked his interest in Geri, and he will reply, "She was beautiful, funny, and when I asked her out, she said yes instead of no." A good start for any relationship.

They did encounter some problems along the way. When Augie was eighteen but Geri still underage, her parents thought things were getting out of hand between them, and Geri was forbidden to see Augie for several months. In the end her parents relented, and to show them that they had made the right decision, Augie decided that he and Geri should talk to her parents together. "To this day," Augie says, "I am not sure why I felt that was necessary or where I found the courage to go through with it, but I think it had a lot to do with how they eventually accepted me back into the family."

When they completed high school, Augie went on to the University of Wisconsin at Milwaukee while Geri worked as a legal secretary. A month after Augie's graduation from college, they had a simple wedding on June 16, 1984, at a local Unitarian church. But there would be no honeymoon. Augie had to start a new job that Monday, and that responsibility came first. They would start their life together in a $150 a month apartment that had no electricity in the bathroom and no kitchen at all. "We knew it could only get better," Augie says.

Partially because they were not going on a honeymoon and were going to be living in such cramped circumstances, Augie gave Geri a handwritten letter on their wedding day that was both an apology and a promise:

Dear Geri,

Although I have looked forward to this day for so very long, it's hard to believe it has actually come. I, of course, need not tell you that there isn't a shred of doubt in me. And I know you feel the same.

Tomorrow we'll wake up and be the same Augie and Geri as always. We'll still love each other just as strongly, we'll still need each other just as much, and we'll be just as committed as always. In fact, the only difference is that we'll both have the same last name. I think this is why I've always been more excited about our marriage than our wedding. Our wedding—a beautiful day, to be sure—will pass, and you and I will be the same. Our marriage, however, is something that we'll live every day and something that will change us continually.

259
•

Our marriage is not starting exactly as I had intended—in a little rundown room with me running off to work. In spite of this, I know we'll be happy. I promise to try to make you happy. I promise that, whenever possible, I'll give you the things you want. I promise to keep you safe. I also promise to love you forever, and that's an easy promise to make.

> *Love always,*
> *Augie*

Augie and Geri have kept that letter in a fireproof box through all their years together. He has always tried to keep the promise to give Geri the things she wants whenever possible, and Geri has reciprocated. Augie loves to tell the story about the watch he saw at a Disney Gallery store when they visited Las Vegas. "I thought it was the coolest thing, but since it was our third day in Lost Wages, and since I had spent my share of time at the tables, I did not feel good about spending a hundred bucks on the watch. We returned to Milwaukee, and every now and then as I passed a jewelry or department store I would look for that same watch, but I never saw it again. Over a year later, I tried to start a business with one of my oldest friends, but it ended badly. I was feeling pretty down but landed a nice job, and on my first day she gave me a gift. It was the watch. Geri had called the store in Las Vegas and had it shipped. I thought that was just the sweetest thing, and I wore it proudly for many years."

On their tenth wedding anniversary, Augie and Geri reaffirmed their vows in a ceremony at Walt Disney World with parents, relatives, and friends—almost two dozen altogether—in attendance. They've now passed their sixteenth anniversary and are planning another ceremony of affirmation for their twentieth. They have attained most of the material things they wanted, but there are deeper, less tangible things to be cherished, too. Augie says that when he takes the letter he wrote Geri on their wedding day out of its fireproof box and rereads it, it sometimes sounds a little naive. But maybe not. The renewal ceremony the two of them wrote together ten years later reflected many of the same feelings about love and romance. Augie thinks they're both still a little naive and idealistic. But how could it be otherwise? They got to know each other because they played the violin, that most romantic of instruments.

There is one kind of letter that no one wants to receive. In England they are called "What If" letters, and in the United States they are usually called "Just in Case" letters. They are most likely to be written by soldiers during wartime, entrusted to a senior officer or good friend, to be delivered only in the event of the writer's death. They can be the most moving kind of letter.

Live for Today

◇

The day after their first wedding anniversary, Gayle received a telegram. *How funny*, she thought as she opened the envelope. *It's late*. No matter, John had been able to get away from the fighting for a few days. He was stationed only hours away from their home in London, and though he had had to return Sunday night they had celebrated just the same. She spent that Monday with her parents and friends, they'd said a toast to her and to John, who'd by then returned to the airfield. And here it was, Tuesday, and she was opening a "Happy Anniversary" telegram a day late! It was sweet of John to try to get it to her on time. She read the telegram:

DEEPLY REGRET TO INFORM YOU THAT YOUR HUSBAND SGT. JOHN HUBBARD ARMSTRONG IS MISSING AS A RESULT OF AIR OPERATIONS ON THE NIGHT OF . . .

Gayle collapsed beside the door.

Now living in Canada, Gayle remembers how, as a teenager growing up in London, England, in the shadow of World War II, she and all her girlfriends adopted the motto "Let's live today as we may never see tomorrow!"

They ran through the city streets, dolled up and ready to dance until they heard the *ack-ack* sound of antiaircraft artillery bursting from the sky. They'd scatter, diving into the nearest doorways as searing scraps of metal smacked against the cobblestones like brutal rain. Then it was on to the roadhouse to jitterbug and fox-trot or maybe the Café de Paris for a rum and Coke.

On Christmas Eve of 1941 a boy in uniform asked Gayle to dance. It wasn't unusual, lots of men asked her to dance. But he was so handsome with his coal-black hair and thin mustache that she accepted without hesitation. They danced the rumba and the tango, Gayle swirling around the dance floor in her mauve evening gown. Gayle was such a skilled seamstress that when she'd seen Loretta Young wearing a similar gown in a film she was able to copy it to a T. After their dance, the officer bought her a glass of wine. His name was John Armstrong, and he was a fighter pilot in the Royal Air Force. The tone of his voice was so smooth and mellow that Gayle found it hard to concentrate on his words. Tennis had been his passion before the war. He'd competed against many and usually left the court victorious. Gayle was also athletic; she had won plenty of medals in swimming and had dreams of becoming a model. Both of their aspirations, however, had been put on hold as the hostilities mounted. He had first volunteered with the Air Raid Precaution Corps before enlisting with the service. She had replaced a man who was called to action and was now working in the offices of British Rail.

It was getting late and the girls had a long walk ahead of them. He would have asked to see her the next night but he was on his way to Florida. His squadron was to complete special training with the U.S. Air Force. Gayle and John promised to meet again upon his return.

Every day brought a new landscape to the London Gayle had always known. Any house could be a pile of bricks by dawn, any neighbor a memory. One night at a local pub Gayle stepped into the powder room and saw a woman from the neighborhood washing her hands at one of the sinks. Gayle's naturally curly hair had begun to frizz. She dabbed a bit of cold water on her hair then twisted a strand around her finger to revitalize the curl. "Go on, dear," the woman next to her gently urged. "Use warm water. Tomorrow we could be gone!" Though Gayle thought it decadent, she turned on the hot water tap and continued to fix her hair. They shared a silly, intimate giggle as the woman dried her hands and left the bathroom. That night the woman's house was bombed. She perished in the rubble.

John returned to England bearing gifts from the

United States for the girl he hoped to make his sweetheart. Gayle opened the packages and nearly fell over: a pair of nylons and a tube of Max Factor lipstick! He told her about the orange groves in Florida and how his golden voice landed him the duty of reading first-aid announcements on the radio. They danced at the Northbrook that evening and before he returned to the airfield, he asked Gayle to be his girl. How could she say no?

Every night the Royal Air Force sent one thousand bombers to Germany and each evening seventy-five would fail to return. "I'm going to be one of those," John would say as they read the papers. They had been dating for a year and it seemed as though the war would never end. Every six weeks John would receive time off, and he eagerly divided his time between his mother's house and Gayle's. She tried to get John to banish those gruesome thoughts from his head, but his fear of death was steadfast. In March of 1943, he proposed to her. Like the mixture of late-night dancing and air raids, word of marriages and deaths seemed oddly intertwined. Both Gayle's older and younger sister were getting married. The Café de Paris had been reduced to rubble, and Gayle's cousin had been injured when a bomb was dropped on her elementary school. For every happy occasion there was at least one tragedy. It was a lot for a teenage girl to think about. And now she too was being asked to the altar.

Not sure of what to do, Gayle went to her dad for advice. "Do you love him?" her father asked. "Daddy, I like him more than any man I have ever known," Gayle replied, "but I do not know if that is love."

If it was love, then John was her first. He, however, was eight years older than she and had been engaged once before. Not long before John met Gayle, the woman he was to marry ran off with another man. Gayle could not be sure if John loved her, if he was rebounding from his engagement, or if it was his fear of mortality that drove his compulsion to marry.

"Marry me, Gayle," John pleaded on his next leave. "Just give me a year of your life. I'm sure I'm going to be dead by then. If you find that you don't like me, well, we'll get a divorce when the war is over. I need you."

Still unsure if it was true love, she accepted John's proposal. Her aunts and mother donated their war ration coupons for fabric so Gayle could make a dress. They married in June in the garden of their church, a bold move considering the fighting above them, but not before John met his friends for a pint at the Northbrook Pub, gathering what he termed "Dutch courage." The newly-weds spent the evening at the Strand Palace Hotel in the center of London before John had to return to his duties.

Over the next year Gayle came to find love with her husband. Each visit they spent together was sweeter than the last. His mother had been widowed years before and, while John was away, Gayle would visit her often. The couple had plans to get a home of their own once the war was over. Until then, they shared Gayle's room at her parents' home. What had started out as a shaky relationship had blossomed into a wonderful romance. The night before their first anniversary, she kissed John good-bye for the last time. Two days later, her husband was missing.

Weeks passed and still there was no word about John. Gayle began to accept the bitter truth that he was dead. She thought about the night he asked for just a year of her life, how he promised they could get a divorce if it didn't work out. Well, she had given him a year and she wanted a hundred more! It *had* worked out and now there was no alternative but to live without him. What was even harder to accept than the telegram, than the weeks of waiting, was the delivery of a box of John's personal effects. Among other things, the box contained a silver pen she had given him and two letters. The first was written on the night of their anniversary, the night he didn't return. In it he reminisced about the day they married, then stopped writing to go into the briefing room, where the pilots would receive their plans for the night's activity. The letter was unsigned, still attached to the pad he was writing on, and will forever remain unfinished.

Monday June 14, 1943

My Beloved Gayle,

One year today and I'm away from you in body but not in spirit.

↑ I was flying from 11:45 A.M. till 1 P.M. and all the while was going over the events of this time last year. Waiting with Ken for the Northbrook Pub to open, meeting Jay and Rob, and then gathering "Dutch courage" to brace me for the ordeal!

271
•

My darling, such a lot has happened since then. We've had a lot of real bliss and unhappiness, too. But I think on the whole we've gained a lot. I know neither of us wish that we were single again. That's a lot gained for a start.

I'd like to write more on this subject, but we have to save it for my next long letter for as you will now guess, we're on tonight. No time to settle down but on right away. On the two raids last week we didn't lose any crew, so let's hope tonight will be the same.

I hated leaving you last night, it nearly

*broke my heart. On meeting Roy and his
father, we had a moan which grew
considerably when Roy and Rob joined up.
The most heartfelt groans came from the
married men, who really felt awful. We know
what it is to leave loving wives behind us,
damn it. Ah me!*

*We had a good journey down with 3½
hours sleep till Retford, where we had tea at
the all-night canteen. I'm going to try to
phone you but you'll understand if I don't get
through. If unlucky, I will phone tomorrow
before you get this.*

*I am now going into the briefing room,
usual plans, no doubt. Just a change of
town. Will finish off tomorrow later on
before I go.*

Gayle wept uncontrollably as she read. The next letter was just as painful. Commonly known as a "What If"
letter, it was a farewell he had written in April of that
year to be read only in the case of his death. All the pilots
wrote them, none of their wives wanted to receive them.
It had been left with an officer for safekeeping and it was
now in Gayle's trembling hands.

Monday, April 5, 1943

My Darling Gayle,

As you will read this only if I am killed, I'm leaving it with the officer with a list of my personal kit, copy of which is enclosed.

I want you to know that you are the only true love of my life, the one who means more to me than anyone else in the world.

273

The greatest happiness in my life has been with you. You have made my fondest dreams come true. I know at times I have been bitter and sarcastic. Please forgive me for any pain I have caused you in any way for I really love you so deeply that you mean my whole life. I understand now what real love means and that is to pray that the one you love should be happy. That's what I want for you: to be happy in your life.

Thank you for marrying me, that honor I have occasionally forgotten in moments of stress. On sane and sober reflection, I fully realize it.

You have been so generous in all ways

since we were married, far more than I can ever repay. I only hope that I should be given the chance one day to do so.

Thank you for your great love you have had for me. It has filled my whole life and thank you, my beloved, for just being you. That covers all things.

Fate has carved our career and life together and if we are parted, it is God's will. I just want you to know how I feel about you, in case I don't happen to come back.

Thank your Mum and Dad for their great kindness to me when I have come home on leave, I appreciate that, too. Please convey my gratitude to them both.

Comfort my Mother for me, she's had a hard life and I know she will appreciate it for she is very fond of you.

For yourself, think of our exquisitely happy moments together, but in the future, try to make the best of things. If you want to marry again, I hope that you have a better husband than I have been. May you always have good fortune, health, and happiness. My blessings go with you in all you say and do.

God bless you and keep you safe from harm always.

Your devoted, adoring husband who sends his wholehearted love to his wonderful wife.

> *Good-bye darling,*
> *John*

275
♦

Sometimes letters are written in truly desperate circumstances, hurriedly composed in the hope that it will actually be possible to mail them. Such letters are often marked by a tension between the need to convey the situation as it is and the human impulse to hold on to even the most tenuous belief in the future.

Letters of Hope

∝

A German Jew who had been born in Berlin, Hans Behr and his wife, Edith, had managed to get out of Germany to France when Hitler's intentions toward the Jews became clear in the late 1930s. But in February of 1943, Hans was arrested in Paris by the Nazis and transported from one French concentration camp to another over the next few weeks, before being deported back to Germany. His two teenage children, Anut and Gys, had already been sent away to camps. Hans was able to send several postcards to Edith as he was transported between the concentration camps at Drancy, Gurs, and Nexon in France. Then, in the last days of February, he was able to write the following letter.

My Beloved Edith!

I don't know if you received already my card from Gurs [a camp at the French-Spanish border] of yesterday. I hardly think so, and therefore my preparing you for the horrible thing (to come) becomes obsolete. My writing is very bad because I am writing on a moving train. Things are not too good

now. So, yesterday we arrived in Gurs
together with many other transports, from
other departments but also from other camps,
which is very striking. I still refused to believe
the unthinkable, but without any selection or
doctor's tests, we were put onto trucks at
night and brought to Oloron [a small town
near the camp at Gurs]. I am sitting now in
the infamous cattle car, which is not all that
bad. We are lying on hay and get sardines,
salami, and figs to eat. But all this is just
secondary. I would prefer to eat nothing and
be at home! Together with me are [some
names of friends]. My darling, darling Edith,
no one could have foreseen all that!
Therefore please do not reproach yourself
that we should have done this or done
that . . . First the children and then I myself.
And yet, as I wrote you before from Gurs—I
am content that it had to be me and not you.
And I'll tell you why. I could never be
without you, I would die. But you are
stronger and have more energy and you will
live through these times . . . And I will endure

in the hope of one day being together again with you and the children. It is easier for the person affected directly than to have to sit by passively and wait . . .

. . . But our separation will not last forever. Other families are separated through continents. Let us hope we will be separated only by long train trips. When will that day arrive? But it will come. I feel it. I know it. Only by then you must look exactly as you do now: young, lively, and with dark hair. After thirty-three years of marriage I shall not write a declaration of love, but I hope that you know—even if I could not say it out loud because of my inhibitions—that I could never have been married to any other woman, and certainly not have had such a long-lasting marriage. I could never have imagined anyone but you as my wife. I know you feel the same way but you were able to say it. And I could not . . .

281

I kiss you,
Your Hans

That was the next-to-last communication Edith would receive from her husband. A final note was dated March 3, 1943.

My Dearest Edith,

So tomorrow we are leaving, destination still unknown. This is my last sign of life, for the moment. We [prisoners] are all together. . . . We are all courageous. I am in good health and hope that our separation will not last too long. Remain strong and courageous as always. I want to see you again unchanged: not in your nerves, not in your heart, not in your hair! Take good care of yourself! This is in both our interests! I hope that in the meantime you have reassuring news from our good children. Halle [code name for himself] told me he wrote to his wife twice. Truly I am not as unhappy as before, hoping to get work maybe even in my profession. There are cases like mine and they wrote they are relatively content. My darling this will be a long and sad separation but that, too, will pass, I am sure. And our future

*life together will be good and happy, as happy
an end to our lives as the past thirty-three
years have been.*

   I embrace and kiss you a thousand times,

Hans

283
◆

   These cards and letters were translated and anno-
tated by Gys Landsberger, the daughter of Hans and
Edith Behr, who survived the war and emigrated to the
United States. She donated her father's letters to the
archives of the Holocaust Museum in Washington, D.C.,
in 1997.

People save love letters, or try to. Eventually the letters from the beginning of the relationship may get put in a box, usually a nice one, a fancy candy box, something gold or silver, and they are put in a closet. From time to time the box may be taken out, and the couple will have a winter evening by the fire reliving old times. But sometimes boxes of letters disappear. On the other hand, boxes of letters can sometimes reappear again, years later, as if by magic.

Lost and Found

Every now and again, the box would come out of the closet—the box containing the letters Gloria Jean had written to her soldier boyfriend Gerry when she was nineteen. They would reread the letters, share a laugh at the town gossip of years ago, marvel at the innocence of two people who barely knew each other. The whereabouts of Gerry's letters to her, on the other hand, were a mystery. Gloria Jean and Gerry thought the letters might turn up when they moved from Massachusetts to Rhode Island, but they were nowhere to be found. The couple presumed the letters were lost. Still, at least one side of their early romance had survived.

When Gerry passed away in 1993, Gloria Jean moved once again. As she packed, she looked for the box of letters she had written to Gerry but she couldn't find them—they were gone, too. "It was just the strangest thing," she says, "I packed my entire house and never found them. It was as if he took my letters with him." What came next was just as peculiar: considered lost for more than thirty years, the letters Gerry had written to her now reappeared out of nowhere.

As a teenager, Gloria Jean would see Gerry coming down the block and think, *Here's that jerk again.* "Hi cousin!" Gerry always said, making reference to the fact they shared the same last name. There were plenty of people in the world with the last name Roy, it wasn't *that* funny. But Gloria Jean would just give a smile and say hello until the next time they saw each other and the same thing would happen all over again.

Irritated or not, Gloria Jean was always ready to dance up a storm. So when she saw Gerry a couple of years later at Peggy's, one of the local hot spots, she danced with him. He was in the army then and home on leave. They were both on dates with other people, so hitting the floor together didn't mean anything anyway. He wasn't a bad dancer, but, truth be told, he couldn't do the cha-cha. They twirled around the dance floor, Gloria Jean's blond ponytail swinging about her shoulders, the jukebox blaring Frankie Avalon's newest single. As for Gerry, never mind that he was on a date with someone else, Gloria Jean captured his imagination. He went back to the army base that night with a new song in his heart.

From then on, every time he was on leave, Gerry took Gloria Jean dancing or bowling. Both were excellent bowlers, always competing to see who would get the first "turkey," their word for three strikes in a row. She wrote letters to Gerry at Fort Bragg telling him who she'd seen at Peggy's or at the Lincoln Park Ballroom and would catch him up on all the news of New Bedford, Massachusetts. On one of his visits home, she taught him how to cha-cha, but never once did she stop to think that they were falling in love. The boys on the base knew better. They saw how Gerry's face would light up every time he received an envelope with her handwriting. "Forget about it, Roy," they would tease, "she's probably found a Jody," meaning another boy, a boy behind his back. Whether it was true or not, Gerry just couldn't take it anymore. Gloria Jean had to be his.

"What's wrong?" Gloria Jean asked when Gerry pulled the car over. They were having a good time just like they always did when Gerry was on leave, but he'd been acting funny the whole day.

"There's something I want to show you," he said, fiddling with his mustache. "It's in the glove box."

Perplexed, she opened the little door and there among the maps and extra pens was a diamond engagement ring. She picked it up slowly, mesmerized by its delicate sparkle. "You gotta be kidding me," she said, her lips barely moving.

"I want you forever, Gloria Jean."

She pulled her gaze away from the ring long enough to lose herself in Gerry's hazel eyes. "You do?"

That night at the Lincoln Park Ballroom, Gloria Jean didn't have to report on any big news. She *was* the big news. "It was meant to be!" one of her girlfriends screamed in delight. "You won't even have to change your name!" Gloria Jean politely smiled. She still didn't think it was that funny.

The wedding date was set for May 3. That gave them a little more than a year to plan. The army, however, had a plan of its own. Gerry received orders to go to Europe that May. Since he couldn't very well miss his own wedding, the date was moved up to January. Gloria Jean had always been an avid correspondent when it came to Gerry and now that they were going to be married, Gloria Jean made her letters extra special by adding a few dashes of scented powder to the pages. Not one to be outdone, Gerry always put the stamps on the envelopes upside down, an age-old tradition that lets the receiver know what they are about to read is a love letter. In this epistle to his bride to be, Gerry writes about moving the wedding date and vividly describes just how much he loves her.

March 27, 1963

Hi There My Love,

How is my wife to be? I hope you are feeling fine. As for me, I'm in love with you so much that I don't sleep nights. Today I

received a letter from you and boy did I read
it and read it and I guess I'll read it till I die.
So you're going bowling tonight. I hope you
get a turkey! As for me, I'm going to just lie
here thinking of you. Since I came back to the
base, I've been thinking that this is all a
dream. I'm so glad you changed our wedding
date because I just can't wait to be near you
forever. Just let me know the date and I'll
arrange the time to go home. I'll be there even
if I have to go AWOL.

   Honey, what did you drop on your letter?
A whole box of powder? I put it in my locker
and boy every time somebody comes close they
think I've got you in my locker. I can't wait till
Saturday when the captain comes and inspects
the barracks! But I just love it. The scent
makes me feel close to you. I want to be home
so I can put the lights out with you in my
arms. I love the part that you wrote to me and
said that your love will always be devoted to
me. I know our love will last and last.

   Do you know how much love I have for
you? Well, it's like this . . . if you were to fill St.
Anthony's church from the basement to the

*steeple with rice and everyday a robin came by
and took one grain of rice away . . . well, that
is how much I love you. Eternity. Darling,
believe me, you are the only one for me.*
Love always and always and always,

292

Your hubby to be,
Gerry

Gerry's orders to go overseas were mysteriously canceled, possibly because he was the only son in his family, though he was never sure exactly why. The January date, however, was already set. "You tricked me!" her father said, not ready to see his little girl leave home. It turned out to be a blessing in disguise, for Gloria Jean's grandmother passed away on May 3, their original wedding date. But even before that, there was one death that the entire country would mourn.

November 22, 1963

Hi Love,

*Well, guess who? Yes, you're right. It's me,
Gerry, the guy who loves you very much. Well,
love, today has been a fair day, the weather is*

*warm here. I'm okay. But today is such a
tragedy. I can't believe it, the terrible death of
our President John Kennedy. Today at 2:30
P.M., they called off the inspection for
tomorrow. Instead, they are having a parade,
the entire post. We're also having a sixty-gun
salute for President Kennedy. He was a great
man. I wish I was half as good and great.
Darling, excuse me today. I have so much on
my mind, but I know things will get better. I
received a nice letter from you today and I
love you but today is so sad. I am a mess. I
don't know what to do. Just stick with me for I
need you more now than ever.*

*Well, my love, I will close for tonight. My
mood is bad and I feel so much sorrow. I will
feel much better tomorrow. May God bless
you and keep you in his care.*

*Love forever,
Gerry*

The two married in January at Saint Killian's
Church in New Bedford. There wasn't much time for a

293

honeymoon for Gerry was due back at the base in a few days. The couple planned a winter tour around New England. On their first evening as husband and wife, they anxiously drove to Boston, checked into a fine hotel, and slipped into something more comfortable. That night, the newlyweds did what they so desperately, passionately wanted to do . . . they went bowling!

It wasn't too long after the wedding, however, that Gloria Jean had to retire her bowling shoes, at least for a while. They were expecting a baby. Since he was the only boy among sisters and female cousins, Gerry and his family prayed for a boy to carry the Roy name. They got their wish. Gerry and Gloria Jean had a baby boy. In the hospital room, her father-in-law shouted, "Thank you, Gloria!" and planted a big kiss on her cheek, ecstatic that the Roys would carry on. In a few years they had another boy, then another, and with each delivery, Gloria Jean's father-in-law was there to thank her. It was an amazing time for Gloria Jean and Gerry. More than husband and wife, they were best friends. They had so much love for each other and their family and still, Gloria Jean wanted to give more.

She snipped the article from the paper and handed it to Gerry, who read with great interest. The article was about becoming foster parents. According to the article, they had everything a foster child could need: a stable environment, a life of happiness, a strong marriage. Having long since left the military, Gerry now worked as a store manager and was home every evening while Gloria Jean only worked part time. Within a year they had two foster sons, ages seven and twelve. Eventually, they adopted the boys. Again, her father-in-law thanked her.

Along with the joy the children brought them came a fair amount of frustration, though Gerry could handle just about any situation with humor. Every evening the boys were expected to set the table and every evening it didn't get done. While the kids sat glued to *The Brady Bunch* one night their dad served up the spaghetti— without plates or silverware. The boys came to the dining room and found five piles of steaming pasta right on the tabletop. "I thought this must be the way you like it," he said with a straight face. From then on, the table got set.

Life went on for the Roys with the usual mixture of highs and lows, though nothing could prepare them for May of 1986. It was then that Gerry went to the doctor complaining of abdominal pain. After many tests, he was diagnosed with mesothelioma, a rare form of cancer, the direct result of exposure to asbestos. They had been able to handle so many things in life, but this was out of their control. With tears staining her face, Gloria Jean went to her parish priest. He allowed her time alone in the church. She had been married to this won-

295

derful man for more than twenty years and all she wanted was one more. A year during which they could spend time alone, travel to the places they'd always wanted to go. Gloria Jean prayed like she had never prayed before. If she could have this year, she promised to let him go the next. The following day he had surgery to remove the tumors that had developed in his abdomen. There was very little chance the procedure would lengthen his life expectancy, but it was the only chance they had. Gerry made it through the surgery and astonished the doctors with his steady recovery—so much so he became known as "Miracle Man" around the hospital. The couple had been preparing for Gerry's death, but now they were ready to live.

Each new day was a gift and they enjoyed that gift to the fullest. Instead of worrying if they could afford to eat out, they would just get in the car and go. Whereas before they "didn't have time" to travel, now they booked a trip to Montreal, and Las Vegas. And California, Mexico, Pennsylvania. "We crammed fifteen years of living into five," she says. "I tell people now, 'Don't wait until you retire. Do it now!'" For years Gerry was cancer free. Then, in 1993, the disease spread to his lungs. Within months he was confined to a wheelchair and wearing an oxygen mask. A hospital bed was moved into the Roys' home. Gerry's time in this life was coming to an end and there was nothing she could do. She had prayed for another year and was blessed with six more. "Will you wait for me at the gate?" she wept. "I will wait for you with open arms," he whispered, "as long as you stay behind for a while." "But you'll only be fifty-four," she said with a mixture of laughter and tears, "I'll be an old lady."

The next morning Gloria Jean awoke and took a shower. As she dressed, a feeling rushed through her. Something told her she needed to be with her husband right that second. She rushed to his bedside and Gerry opened his eyes, the same beautiful hazel eyes she'd looked at in bewilderment when she found the engagement ring in the glove box of his car. He looked so youthful that it gave Gloria Jean a sudden burst of relief and joy. "Hi Gerry!" she chirped. He put his hand on hers, closed his eyes, and was gone.

When Gloria Jean found Gerry's letters, she had to stop packing and read them right then and there. How wonderful and strange, after all those years! With the delight also came the sorrow of his absence, the fact she was leaving the home they had shared. She couldn't go on with packing that day. Instead, she sat down and wrote, something she'd been doing a lot lately.

I took a peek at love letters
from so many years ago.

Words of value and trust
so precious to me, my love.
I paused for a moment
to reread your expressions of love,
pretty notes and special memories
to carry always and to never let go

Four years after Gerry's death, Gloria Jean self-published a collection of her poems to Gerry entitled *The Scent of Flowers*. The book chronicles her journey from grief to healing. "The poems are love letters to Gerry," she says. "He already has the old ones. Now he can have these, too."

There are moments in life when it is difficult to know what to say—when there is a death in the family or when one must face a daunting challenge. But there are those who can not only find the words, but act upon them in ways, large and small, that confirm to the utmost the message of love that has been written in a letter.

In Sickness and in Health
◯—

The ship left Florida bound for Jamaica, and then continued to sail on to Haiti and Mexico. On board, the Seich family, Amy, Bruce, and their two daughters, Jennifer and Lauren, were enjoying all the ship had to offer. They twirled around the roller-blading and ice-skating rinks. They tested their skills on the miniature golf course. Amy cheered her family on as they scaled the giant rock-climbing wall and ventured into the sea for jet skiing. Bruce entered the volleyball competition. They certainly had a lot to celebrate and were doing it in the grandest style. Amy and Bruce toasted twenty years of marriage. Lauren's team had won the state basketball championship and Jennifer had finished her sophomore year of high school with stellar grades. It was also a time to rejoice in the miracle of life. Amy had been cancer free for ten years.

In 1987, Amy went to her doctor complaining about a strange sensation in her breast. "It feels like hot water rushing through me," she told him. Her doctor didn't take the complaint lightly. Amy's father had died of breast cancer some years before, a rare occurrence affecting less than 1 percent of the male population. The doctor ran a series of tests that showed that Amy had microcalcification—harmless pin-sized dots inside her left breast. Amy was only thirty-two years old at the time and in good health. Her doctor told her not to worry but to come back in six months. She did and again the tests were all clear. A year later, she returned for a mammogram. More than a week had passed before the doctor called with the results.

The physician's tone was serious and before he could say anything else, she asked Bruce to pick up the bedroom phone. Once her husband was on the line with them, the doctor told her the news: her left breast was inundated with cancer. After a moment, she asked the first of many questions to come. "Am I going to die?" "We're going to do everything to make sure that doesn't happen," the doctor replied. That wasn't exactly the no she wanted to hear. Amy held the phone to her ear, hearing the words and comprehending nothing. She dropped the receiver and ran outside, her face wet with tears. She sat on a rock in front of her home and drew her knees into her chest. *How can they be so normal?* she thought as people walked passed. *How can their lives go on?* Bruce came to her side and held her. When she finally had the strength to get up, they went indoors.

For days Amy was numb to everything around her. Friends and family came to visit, though their actions seemed more like a movie she was watching than real life. Conflicting emotions churned inside of her; one minute she was scared, the next hurt or angry. She found herself blaming her father for her troubles—as if it were his fault he had contracted cancer, his fault he had died, and his fault that now she was faced with her own mortality. So many decisions had to be made in a short amount of time. Breast cancer thrives on hormones and, since Amy was premenopausal, time was of the essence. Before she could think about doctors and treatments, there was one obligation she had to fulfill: her daughter Jennifer's fifth birthday. Now more than ever, Amy felt she needed to give her daughter a memorable party. That giving instinct in herself was encouraging. Now wasn't her time to die. Too many people needed her.

303
•

She sought a second opinion and then another and another until she had gone to five different doctors. Four suggested a mastectomy, though one thought she would benefit from chemotherapy. She chose chemotherapy. Before she went in for her first treatment, Bruce wrote her the following letter.

Amy,

   I have always tried to be your white knight in shining armor, but this current situation is a little out of my reach in the role

of the hero. However, from what I have seen
you are handling this as well as anyone could.
I will still be here to help you, support you,
and do whatever I can to get you and us
through this. We have always been a team,
that's the key to our relationship—
togetherness. This time you will be out front
fighting and I'm going to be there in your
corner urging you on and helping figure out
the best way to conquer the enemy. This is a
fight, a battle . . . possibly the toughest we have
faced, but we have a lot of love, a lot of years,
and we are one tough team. Your family and
mine and our friends will all be here as they
have been so far. For us. Don't forget the key to
our team is "u." You are the one up front and
none of us can change that, but we will not let
you be alone, now or ever. We all love you and
our love can beat anything. We will do this
and we will continue on and be stronger
together because of it.

I love you, the girls love you, your family
and friends love you.

Bruce

They had started out as college sweethearts and had been married nearly ten years. More than partners, in Bruce's eyes, he and Amy were one. Never before had this been more evident than when Amy went into treatment. Determined to take the best possible care of his wife and their daughters, he quit his job as an accountant. He looked after the girls while Amy slept and arranged for a friend or relative to sit with them if she had a doctor's appointment so he could go with her. The girls never missed a day of school, and their teachers were getting to know Bruce as well as they had known Amy. Though the battle had barely begun, Amy knew she was not alone. All of her neighbors turned up at her house one afternoon, each holding a different cleaning implement. Ignoring her protests, everyone took a room and the entire house was clean within an hour. Hundreds of cards and letters flooded the Seich mailbox. Words of support poured in from the principal of her daughter's school, distant relatives, and people she barely knew. Whenever she went to the mailbox and found another note of encouragement, it lent her strength. Other days, however, were not so bright.

Amy developed psychoneurological nausea, a condition that causes people to vomit at any mention of medical treatment. Driving past a hospital or even seeing a nurse on television could send her running for the bathroom. She lost her hair twice due to the chemotherapy. After one treatment, her veins collapsed. It was becoming increasingly clear, moreover, that she would have to have a mastectomy.

Needing the support of people in the same situation, Amy joined a group for breast cancer patients. As she and Bruce walked into their first meeting, Amy looked around the room. There were about a dozen women in various stages of recovery. What shocked her wasn't the fact that she was one of the youngest in the group or that there were others without hair, it was the realization that Bruce was the only man among them. *Where are their husbands?* she thought. *Where are their boyfriends?* When it came time to introduce himself, Bruce said, "I'm Bruce, Amy's husband, and I'm a co-cancer patient. Amy has cancer, so I have half of it." She was mesmerized by her husband as he spoke to the group. He loved her no matter how she looked or felt. His words were the most cherished gift she'd ever received. No matter what the outcome, she would always see herself as a very lucky woman. The feeling only intensified over the following weeks as she became more intimate with the support group.

Whereas Bruce had done hours of research, the other women recounted the reluctance of their husbands to learn anything about the disease. One of the older women hadn't even told her husband when she went in for surgery. A younger woman spoke about her fiancé calling off the wedding soon after her diagnosis. But Bruce remained steadfast throughout the ordeal. After the mastectomy and reconstructive surgeries, Bruce was there to change the dressings, fix the drains that took fluids from her lymph nodes, and feed her until she was ready to come home.

307

It had been a year since she was first diagnosed with breast cancer. Nine months of chemotherapy, five surgeries, countless bone scans and blood work, and she had survived. She had been so caught up in getting better, Amy hadn't stopped to think about everyday living. It had been a year since Bruce quit his job to take care of her. How did they still have a roof over their heads and food in the refrigerator? One word said it all: family. "You mean to tell me Auntie Ida paid our mortgage last month?" she asked her husband in bewilderment. "Our parents paid the bills? Uncle George gave you a check?" There wasn't a member of her family who hadn't done what he or she could. Bruce was right, they were one tough team.

Four months after her final surgery Amy's hair had yet to return. She had purchased a wig for going outdoors and wore scarves while inside to keep away the draft. Late one hot August evening, Amy broached a subject that hadn't come up between herself and her husband in a long time. "You want to fool around?" she asked quietly. Her husband smiled. "We'd been married over ten years, had been through so much together, and I was suddenly self-conscious about my appearance," Amy says now. "I asked him, 'Do you want the hair?' He said he did and I just felt awful. Here I was, bald as a cue ball, thinking, *I'm not pretty to him anymore.* So I put the wig on and he looked at me and said, 'What are you doing?' 'I asked you if you wanted the hair . . . ' 'I thought you said air!' Bruce exclaimed. He wanted me to turn on the air conditioning! He didn't care what I looked like! He just loved me."

Ask Amy what the sunset from the cruise ship was like and she won't tell you it was the most beautiful she's ever seen. In her eyes, every sunset is precious. The flowers are brighter, the sky the most brilliant shade of blue. She is thankful for every day, for every person who sent her a card, for her family's support, and for Bruce's unwavering love. In the years she has been cancer free, Amy and Bruce have raised thousands of dollars for breast cancer research. Though no longer a member of the support group, she now counsels others facing the same set of obstacles. "Just because I'm cancer free doesn't mean I've stopped worrying," she says. "I go for checkups every year and my daughters are going to have to be brutally aware of the dangers"—though worries were far from their minds while aboard the ship. Bruce took first place in the volleyball tournament and the whole family took second prize in miniature golf. And, as Amy says, "Family is everything."